The Earliest Recorded Bridge at Rochester

Colin Flight

BAR British Series 252
1997

Published in 2019 by
BAR Publishing, Oxford

BAR British Series 252

The Earliest Recorded Bridge at Rochester

© Colin Flight and the Publisher 1997

ISBN 9780860548485 paperback
ISBN 9781407318806 e-book

DOI https://doi.org/10.30861/9780860548485

A catalogue record for this book is available from the British Library

This book is available at www.barpublishing.com

BAR Publishing is the trading name of British Archaeological Reports (Oxford) Ltd.
British Archaeological Reports was first incorporated in 1974 to publish the BAR
Series, International and British. In 1992 Hadrian Books Ltd became part of the BAR
group. This volume was originally published by Tempvs Reparatvm in conjunction
with British Archaeological Reports (Oxford) Ltd / Hadrian Books Ltd, the Series
principal publisher, in 1997. This present volume is published by BAR Publishing,
2019.

BAR
PUBLISHING

BAR titles are available from:

BAR Publishing
122 Banbury Rd, Oxford, OX2 7BP, UK
EMAIL   info@barpublishing.com
PHONE   +44 (0)1865 310431
FAX   +44 (0)1865 316916
www.barpublishing.com

Contents

Acknowledgements

My thanks, first of all, go to Nicholas Brooks, for the stimulus provided by two recent publications, both of which he was kind enough to let me see in advance, and for his comments on a draft of the present paper.

I should also like to express my gratitude to the archivists and librarians whose help I have relied on during the writing of this report, in particular to Dr James M. Gibson (Rochester Bridge Trust), Bernard Nurse (Society of Antiquaries), and Elizabeth A. Walsh (Folger Shakespeare Library, Washington, D.C.).

The report of an official inquiry held at Rochester on 12 June 1355 (below, pp. 52-3) is printed from the transcript in the Thorpe Bequest (MS. 198/1, part II, fol. 151) by permission of the Society of Antiquaries of London.

List of figures

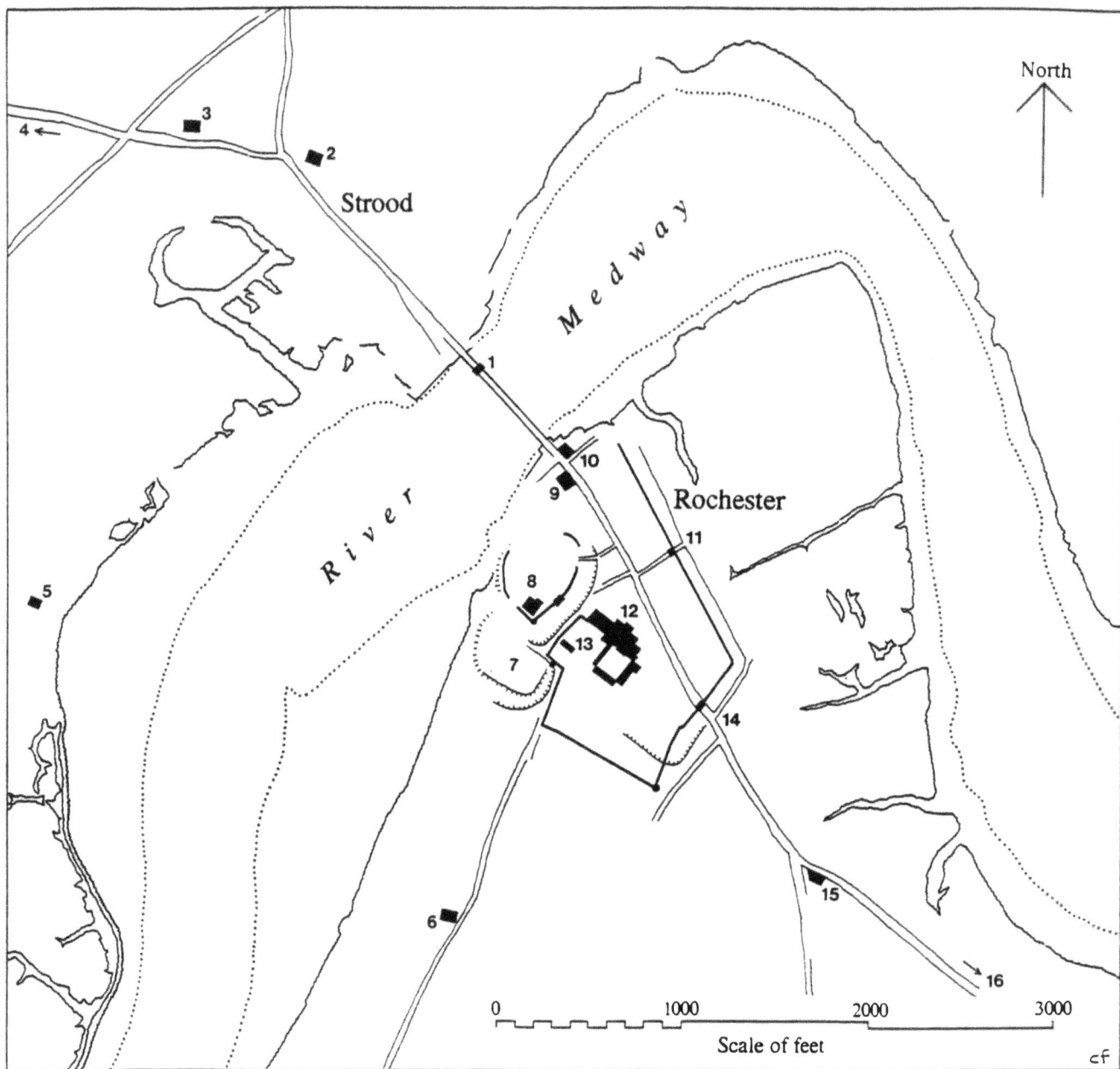

Fig. 1. The topography of Rochester in the mid fourteenth century. (1) Barbican on the bridge, (2) Hospital of Saint Mary called the New Work, (3) Strood church, (4) Hospital of Saint Nicholas called White Ditch, (5) Temple Manor, (6) Saint Margaret's church, (7) Boley Hill, (8) Castle, (9) Crown Inn, (10) Saint Clement's church, (11) *Cheldegate*, (12) Cathedral church and monastery of Saint Andrew, (13) Bishop's hall, (14) Eastgate, (15) Hospital of Saint Katherine, (16) Hospital of Saint Bartholomew.

1

Introduction

Three successive bridges − three that we know about − have carried the main road from east Kent to London across the river Medway between Rochester and Strood (Fig. 1). The earliest recorded bridge, existing in the twelfth century and probably long before, survived until the fourteenth century. It was abandoned in the 1380s and superseded by a new bridge built on a different site, just a short distance upstream. The fourteenth-century bridge survived − not without some important alterations − until the nineteenth century.[1] It was abandoned in the 1850s and superseded in its turn by a new bridge built on a different site, just a short distance downstream − almost exactly the same site as that of the earliest bridge. Alongside the new roadbridge, on the downstream side, a railway bridge was constructed, also in the 1850s, by the East Kent Railway Company (which shortly afterwards changed its name to 'London Chatham & Dover'); alongside that a second railway bridge was built in the 1880s, by the rival South Eastern company.[2] The three nineteenth-century bridges are all in existence today, though two of them have undergone some drastic modifications since they were first built.[3]

All these bridges − including the railway bridges − have their share of archaeological interest, but here I propose to deal only with the oldest among them, the bridge which reached the end of its useful life in the 1380s. There are no hard facts. Some discoveries made in the 1850s, during the construction of the new roadbridge, were put on record by the engineer responsible (below, pp. 32-4), but their significance is far from clear. With that one doubtful exception, no part of the actual structure has been identified. On the Rochester side at least, some remains of the abutment may quite possibly survive; but if they do they underlie the approach to the modern bridge, and are likely to remain hidden for as long as that bridge continues to exist. In the absence of structural evidence, we have to do the best we can with the information contained in written sources.

The ideal evidence, I suppose, would be a set of itemized accounts relating to the repair of some specified portion of the bridge, recording exactly what materials were used, and exactly what they were used for. Though none of the surviving documents come close to that ideal, there are several which provide us with useful information.

The bridgework text

Of all the available documents, by far the most important is also the earliest. The original was − or so it seems safe to assume − a separate document preserved in the archive of the church of Rochester. It does not survive; but there is one copy in existence.

This solitary copy occurs in a cartulary compiled in the 1120s, under the title 'Privileges granted to the church of Saint Andrew of Rochester', *Priuilegia aecclesiae sancti Andreae Hrofensis concessa*.[4] The compiler was a member of the monastic community which since the 1080s had been attached to the church of Rochester, and the cartulary mostly consists of documents dating from within the previous forty or fifty years. The opening section, however, which forms a booklet by itself, comprises a series of older documents − some as old as the eighth century − which the monks would have found in the church's archive when they first arrived. It is here, at the end of this booklet, that the scribe made his copy of the document concerning the bridge.

As is true for two other documents included in this booklet (Campbell 1973, nos. 34-5), two versions of the text are given: a Latin version and an English version. (The reader will find a line-for-line transcription of both versions in Appendix 1, and may perhaps like to glance through it at this point.) It seems to be a fair assumption, in every case, that the English version was the original one, and that the Latin version was translated from it − at a time, presumably, when documents written in English were at risk of being not understood, or not taken seriously.[5] Though we cannot be sure, these Latin versions are likely to have had some prior existence (perhaps in single-sheet form) before they were copied into the cartulary. Though often helpful, they have to be treated cautiously: the translation is

1

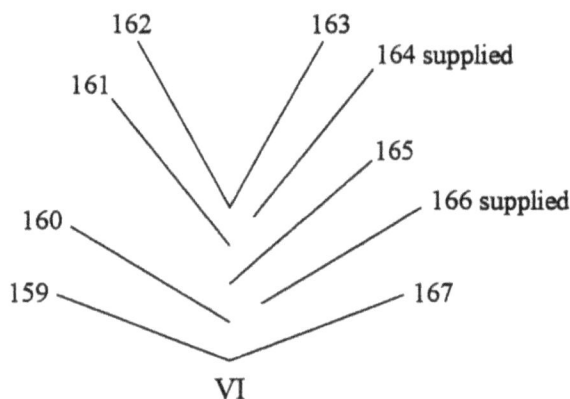

Fig. 2. The quire containing the bridgework text
(*Privilegia*, fols. 159-167).

sometimes very loose, and sometimes plainly wrong. The Latin version of the bridgework text is certainly something more than a mere translation: a whole paragraph occurs at the end of it which has no counterpart in the English version.

Like some other portions of the cartulary, the leaves containing the bridgework text underwent mutilation at the hands of later scribes; and to understand the significance of their actions we need to look more closely at the relationship between the text itself and the leaves on which it is written. When it was being photographed for the purpose of being published in facsimile, the manuscript was disbound and disassembled; so we know exactly how the pieces fit together (Sawyer 1962). The leaves containing the bridgework text belong to quire VI, which consists of nine leaves in total (fols. 159-167, Fig. 2).[6] Two of the leaves in question are not original, as Ker (1957, p. 447) was the first to point out: two leaves have been excised, and these two have been inserted in their place.[7]

Briefly, the facts are as follows. The recto of the first inserted leaf (fol. 164) is blank. On the verso we find the beginning of the Latin version of the bridgework text, written by a hand assigned by Ker to the late twelfth or early thirteenth century. The remainder of the text (beginning with *gisleardes lande*),[8] on the following leaf (fol. 165), is in the main hand. It occupies the whole recto and half of the verso, where it is followed by twelve blank lines. Next is the second inserted leaf (fol. 166), which again is blank on the recto. On the verso we find the beginning of the English version, in a hand of about the same date as that of fol. 164 (though surely

not the same hand). Here again the text is continued, on the following leaf (fol. 167), in the main hand (beginning with *wroteham*). It ends near the bottom of the recto; the verso was left blank. This leaf is the last of its quire, and the last of the booklet (quires I-VI) containing pre-conquest documents.

Looking more closely at the rewritten portion of the Latin version (fol. 164v), we can more or less work out what has happened. The first third of the page (as far as *supponere* at the beginning of line 8) looks like an imitation − clumsily written but passably convincing − of the hand of the main scribe. Up to this point, the later scribe seems to be giving us a facsimile of the page which he is replacing.[9] From this point onwards (beginning with an unnecessary capital letter, *Et hoc faciet*) the writing changes, presumably because the scribe has stopped trying to imitate the earlier script. Here, it seems, he starts to copy from a different exemplar, trying to fit some new wording into the space available on the rest of this page. The text has a cramped appearance, especially in the last two lines, where the scribe begins to realize that he is running out of room: his writing here has a very different appearance from the well-spaced rounded script with which he started.

In the rewritten portion of the English version (fol. 166v), the script is broadly similar to that of the main scribe, though more cursive, and not so neat; but in detail the differences are clear (in the shape of æ, for instance, or of the 7-like symbol for *and*, or in the treatment of the downward strokes of f and similar letters). By and large, the scribe seems at ease with the script: insular forms of letters like f and g and special characters like wen and thorn flow smoothly from his pen, without more than the occasional hesitation to which any copyist is liable. On the other hand, there are signs that he was finding the language hard to handle. Small errors and inconsistencies, though not confined to this portion of the text, are distinctly more numerous here. This scribe, it appears, was accustomed to writing English, but not the archaic sort of English found in the bridgework text.[10]

In both versions, therefore, we find that a portion of the text was copied out again by a later hand. Some care was taken to ensure that the rewritten portion would link up neatly with the original portion on the following page, though in neither case was this intention perfectly achieved. From the fact that the rewritten sections of the text include the two segments of the bridge for which the bishop of Rochester was responsible (segments 1 and 3), it seems tolerably certain that the arrangements relating to these two segments were being modified, and that the text was written out again to take account of these changes (below, p. 11).

Before the excision of these two leaves, the text had already been amended to reflect some change in the arrangements relating to segment 4, the segment which belonged to the king. In the Latin version there is a long erasure in the list of places liable for work on this segment. In the rewritten portion of the English version there is a corresponding blank;[11] it seems that the scribe deliberately left a lacuna at this point, to imitate an erasure on the page that he was recopying, and that implies that the names had been erased before the beginning of the thirteenth century.

By a fortunate but puzzling accident (below, p. 4), the missing names turn up – as Ward (1934, p. 13) was first to observe – in a document from Canterbury. There are four of them: Loose, Linton, Stockenbury, and one which cannot be identified.[12] The three identifiable places are among the most southerly places named in the text; it seems a likely guess that they were excused from contributing to Rochester bridge because they had been made responsible for a different bridge somewhere closer (possibly at Yalding). Though the Rochester monks were capable of many tricks where their own property was concerned, they did not have any interest in these places; so it is not to be thought that the names were erased secretly by them, for some selfish reason. On the contrary, I think we have to suppose that this change in the arrangements

had been properly discussed and decided, and that the Rochester monks altered the document in their custody, not from any nefarious motive, but simply for the purpose of bringing it up to date.[13]

The significance of these alterations has to be largely a matter of speculation, but the mere fact that such changes were made is proof that this document was not a dead letter. It was consulted; it was accepted as having authority. Indeed, the same view of it was taken by the original scribe, who treated it in a special way, unlike all the other documents in this booklet. Both versions of the text begin right at the top of a verso page: this is true of them in their rewritten form, and must surely have been true of them also in their original form. Thus one can start to read as soon as one opens the book, without having to scan through the end of some preceding document.[14] The scribe was so determined to achieve this layout that he was willing to sacrifice a large amount of space, leaving whole pages blank; he was also obliged to include an extra leaf (fol. 165) which would otherwise not have been needed. In short, he expected that people would want to consult this document, and did his best to make things easy for them.

To summarize what has been said so far: in the 1120s, when we first become aware of it, the text existed in its English version as a copy in *Privilegia* and probably also as a single sheet, and in its Latin version as a copy in *Privilegia* and possibly also as a single sheet. There seems to be no reason for thinking that any other copy existed, in Rochester or anywhere else. At some point in the mid or late twelfth century, the copies in *Privilegia* were altered by erasure, but we cannot say what happened to the single sheets. Around 1200, the copies in *Privilegia* were both partly rewritten, but again we cannot say what happened to the single sheets.[15]

After that, as far as we know, the English version was not reproduced again until the sixteenth century. The Latin version, however, was transcribed at least four times.[16] Two copies occur in later manuscripts from Rochester (below, p. 51). Later still, two copies cited by Brooks (1994, p. 364) survive among the records of central government: they date from the 1390s, and relate to the discussion under way at that time regarding the arrangements to be adopted for maintaining the new bridge. The differences between these various copies are, it seems, slight and insignificant.[17]

Other documents

For some hundreds of years, successive versions of the bridgework text were the only written record of the arrangements relating to the maintenance of the bridge. During the thirteenth century, however, new kinds of documentation began to come into existence. More and more, government departments insisted on having their business recorded in writing, and on having the records kept for future reference. From about the 1330s onwards, though the evidence is still patchy, when we put it all together we have what is probably a fairly complete account of the bridge's misadventures, during the last fifty years of its existence.[18] In 1339-40, for example, the bridge was out of action for more than five months, from 14 October till 3 April; and the following documents survive: (1) the king's commission, dated 17 October 1339, authorizing three named men to operate a ferry (copied on the fine roll and also on the patent roll); (2) the account submitted to the Exchequer by these men, itemizing the proceeds from the ferry and the costs which they had incurred; and (3) the report of an inquiry held at Rochester on 1 March 1340 (Appendix 2, no. 4) ascertaining who should pay for the repairs to the fifth segment.[19]

One thirteenth-century document (Appendix 2, no. 1) owes its survival to the monks of Canterbury. Because it became available in print at an early stage (below, p. 5), this text has attained a prominence which it does not really deserve; but it does have some interesting features, enough to justify a rather closer look.[20]

Rather obviously, the text is stratified. Layer 1 is the report of an inquiry which had been instructed to ascertain who was liable for repairing the bridge at Rochester. It seems to date from about 1230.[21] Like others of the same kind, the report is loosely paraphrased from the bridgework text; but it adds some further information in paragraphs 4 and 6. (By paragraph *j* I mean the portion of the text relating to the *j*th segment of the bridge: the paragraphs were numbered like this by Lambarde (1576), when he first put the text into print.) The inquiry had evidently been told to pay special attention to the fourth and sixth segments of the bridge — presumably because these were the segments in need of repair at the time. Layer 2 is an interpolation made at Canterbury, no later than about 1320: it consists of a single paragraph (beginning 'Let it be noted that', *Notandum quod*) which relates specifically to the manor of Hollingbourne. Because of this

interpolation, I refer to the text as the Hollingbourne memorandum.

The additional information provided by this document is of some significance. In paragraph 6 it tells us that the sixth segment of the bridge 'belongs to the hundred of Eyhorne'; and it then supplies a long list of place-names,[22] together with the number of sulungs for which each place was answerable.[23] One of the places appearing in the list is Hollingbourne, which belonged to the monks of Canterbury; and that, no doubt, is why they they thought it worth their while to obtain a copy of the report in question. It was at the end of this paragraph that they added their interpolation, working out the division of responsibility in very much finer detail for their own manor.

In paragraph 4, similarly, the report gives a list of places and a list of assessments, but here it is only the numbers which are new: the place-names have been taken from the bridgework text. In the process, the list has undergone some interesting mutations.[24] First, Aylesford has disappeared — the likeliest reason being (I would guess) that the men of Aylesford now had a bridge of their own to look after, and claimed that they should therefore be excused.[25] Second, six names have been dropped to the end of the list, and for these no assessments are quoted. Of the places in question three are unidentifiable (below, p. 17), and quite possibly their names were just as mysterious in the thirteenth century as they are now. The other three names refer to places which certainly did exist at the time, but perhaps (for one reason or another) they were not separately assessed.

Third, there are four places listed here which do not appear in *Privilegia*. Assessments are quoted for three of them, so it certainly was the intention that these places should be made to pay. As Ward (1934) observed, these names would fit comfortably into the erasure which occurs in *Privilegia* (above, p. 3), and no doubt he was right to infer that these are the missing names. But that poses a problem. The version of the bridgework text lying behind this report agreed with the rewritten portion of the text in paragraphs 1 and 3. It took account of the changes (whatever they were) made around 1200 in those two paragraphs; so how can it fail to take account of the change made earlier than that in paragraph 4? To be fair with the evidence, we are not entitled to accept Ward's theory unless we can think of some solution for this conundrum.[26]

Printed texts

The bridgework text was first put into print by William Lambarde, in his *Perambulation of Kent*, published in 1576.[27] He had copied it himself, directly from the Rochester cartulary – 'an olde volume of Rochester Librarie, ... entituled, *Textus de Ecclesia Roffensi*' (Lambarde 1576, p. 303). The English version (pp. 307-11) was printed in a quasi-Anglo-Saxon typeface, and accompanied by an interlinear translation into contemporary English. Reversing the order of the manuscript, Lambarde put the Latin version second (pp. 311-12), no doubt because it seemed to him (quite rightly) less important.

Though Lambarde was a fine scholar (and a good man), the text which he published of the English version did not give a very accurate idea of the text which appears in the manuscript. There are more than fifty discrepancies. Without saying so, Lambarde emended some of the mistakes occurring in the rewritten portion.[28] As well as these intentional changes, several errors were introduced, either by Lambarde himself or by the printer; and one error in particular – a numeral which ought to be *iii* misprinted as *iiii* – bedevilled the issue for more than 300 years.[29]

The Hollingbourne memorandum too was put into print by Lambarde (1576, pp. 304-6). His own transcript, he explains, 'was taken out of a booke ... belonging to the late ... Doctor Nicholas Wotton,[30] and whiche he had exemplified out of an auncient monument [= muniment] of Christes Church in Canterbury' (p. 303).[31] Though this document is given first, before the two versions of the bridgework text, that does not imply any judgement of its relative importance: it merely reflects the order in which the texts came into his possession.

Though Lambarde had not explored the records of central government, somebody else was doing just that, at just about this time. In 1575 a royal commission was appointed to overhaul the administration of the bridge (Gibson 1994, pp. 127-9). Among other lines of inquiry, it decided that it ought to ascertain which places had been responsible for maintaining the old bridge (since that responsibility had been transferred to the new bridge at the end of the fourteenth century). For this purpose a search was ordered to be made through the government records in the Tower of London, and three relevant documents were discovered – the reports submitted by earlier commissions of inquiry, in 1277, 1343, and 1355 respectively (Appendix 2, nos. 3, 5, 6).[32] From the late sixteenth century onwards, through various channels – notably through Harris's *History of Kent* (1719, pp. 255-6) – some knowledge of these documents was in circulation among Kentish antiquaries.

For a long while, historians wanting to consult the bridgework text, even those who had access to the manuscript, were usually content to look it up in Lambarde. His text was reprinted on several occasions – in subsequent editions of the *Perambulation*, in Harris's *History* (1719), in Hearne's edition of the 'Textus Roffensis' (1720).[33] None of these reprints show any sign of having been checked against the manuscript: they inherit Lambarde's errors and risk adding new errors of their own. Birch (1885-93, vol. 3, p. 659) produced a more accurate edition, but his text is still not fully independent from Lambarde's: it appears to be a copy of Hearne's text (which itself was copied from Lambarde's), very carefully but not quite perfectly collated with the original manuscript.[34] Robertson (1939, pp. 106-9) finally supplied an edition of the English text – the first since Lambarde's – which was based immediately on the manuscript, not on some previous edition. Her text (accompanied by a translation on the facing page) is decidedly the best available in print.[35]

The word 'per'

It is not possible to translate the text, let alone to make sense of it, without first dispelling one chronic misapprehension. The word *per* does not mean 'pier'. It means 'span'. Somebody tried to point this out two hundred years ago, but no one was listening.

The word is a puzzle for the lexicographers. Its etymology is unknown, and the word itself does not occur at all commonly before the seventeenth century.[36] By far the earliest (and the only 'Old English') occurrence of the word is in this Rochester text, where it appears nine times in all.[37] From the use which is made of it here, we can tell that the word was feminine, with nominative singular *per* and accusative singular *peran*.[38]

The corresponding word in the Latin version is *pera*, the history of which is, if anything, more obscure. Without claiming any competence in historical linguistics, I take it to be a safe series of assumptions that *pera* and *per* are related, that the relationship results from borrowing, and that borrowing from Latin into English is more likely than the reverse. That is how Robertson (1939, p. 351) was inclined to interpret the evidence; Brooks (1994, p. 364) says the same, in more decided terms. It seems doubtful whether any definite conclusion can be arrived at; but for present purposes I see no harm in allowing the assumption that English *per* was borrowed from Latin *pera*, as long as two provisos are borne in mind. First, it is not to be thought – what Robertson thought – that the borrowing occurred at some post-conquest date: Brooks is surely right to infer that the word *per* was part of the English lexicon well before 1066. Second, it is not to be taken for granted that the meaning of the English word was the same as that of its Latin parent: not uncommonly, words undergo some shift of meaning in the process of being borrowed. If that much can be agreed on, the remaining questions – where the word came from in the first place, how it entered Latin,[39] how it passed from Latin into English – can cheerfully be left unanswered.

Whatever it means elsewhere, in this context the word *per* has to be construed to mean 'span'. This was recognized in the 1780s, during the exchange of correspondence which resulted in the writing of a paper by James Essex. I discuss the genesis of Essex's paper elsewhere (below, pp. 36-7); here I am concerned with only one of the items in the dossier, a letter from Owen Manning to Richard Gough.[40]

Gough had written to Manning – the editor of what was then the standard Anglo-Saxon dictionary – asking him to clarify the meaning of some of the words which occur in the bridgework text: *syll, gyrd, leccan*. Having looked up the text in Lambarde, Manning replied. In due course he got round to dealing with the questions put to him by Gough; but he began his letter with a comment of his own. This is what he says:

> The first thing observable in respect to this bridge is, that the floor of it consisted of nine unequal portions of planking, to be kept in repair by nine different sets of persons; whence it is plain that what the author of the Text. Roff. calls piers, were not what we call such, viz the supporters, but the intervals between, or what in stone-work we call the arches.

That must be right. The argument is simple; the conclusion seems obvious as soon as it is made explicit.[41] The bridge is described as consisting of nine segments, each of which has associated with it a certain quantity of planking and a certain number of beams. This woodwork goes to form the deck of the bridge. Since the segments are segments of the deck, they correspond with the openings of the bridge, not with its supports. Given that the piers were of stone (below, p. 39), a fact unknown in the 1780s, it becomes all the clearer that the text when it seems to speak of 'piers' is actually referring to the spans.

A derivative word, *landper*, is used with respect to the first and last spans. It looks obvious, and may be true, that the term 'landpier' should properly mean 'abutment'; but that is not the meaning it carries here.[42] In this text a *landper* is one or other of the extreme spans – a span next to an abutment.

While the bridge itself remained in existence, the wording of the text would not have been open to any misunderstanding. Anyone who thought that *per* meant 'pier' could be sent to count the openings for himself. From the thirteenth century onwards, in reports concerning the bridge, the Latin word *pera* was regularly used to mean 'span', and generally no one seems to have thought that any explanation was called for.

There is one report, however, which does betray some anxiety that the wording of the text was at risk of being deliberately misconstrued – that the men of Gillingham and Chatham, say, might try to evade their responsibility for repairing the second span by claiming to be responsible for the second pier. Whoever drafted this report was concerned to block that argument. The first time the word *pera* appears in this text, its meaning is spelt out for us: what is called 'the first pier', we are told very firmly, includes the whole first span.[43] By this time, there was a barbican defending the western end of the bridge (below, p. 41). That could be thought to complicate the interpretation of this report; but I do not see much room for doubt myself. We are told explicitly that there were nine (not eight) spans; and we can safely infer that the barbican stood on top of the original abutment on the Strood side.

By the fourteenth century, therefore, some ambiguity seems to have accrued, either to Latin *pera*, or to English *per*, or to both words equally. In a Rochester context at least, both words had always meant 'span'; but that meaning had come into conflict with another meaning. The first sense still had some currency in Lambarde's time. It is clear, he says, from the documents which he has printed, 'that this auncient bridge consisted of nyne Arches, or peres' (Lambarde 1576, p. 312); and here he is certainly treating the words as synonyms.[44] By the eighteenth century, however, the modern sense was accepted as being the only proper sense, and − as is proved by Manning's remark − it now required some imagination to realize that the word had ever meant anything else.[45] Manning alone saw the light. Unfortunately, his letter was not passed on to Essex, who, like everyone else, continued to take it for granted that *per* meant 'pier'.

Translation

Before proceeding further, the reader may like to consult the following translation. I offer it without any comment, except to explain that the ellipses * * * denote the lists of place-names discussed directly below.

> This is the construction of the bridge at Rochester. Here are named the lands from which it is to be constructed.
> 1   First, the bishop of the town undertakes to construct the landspan on the (east) arm, and (there are) 3 rods to plank and 3 beams to lay. * * *
> 2   Next, the second span belongs to Gillingham and Chatham, and (there is) 1 rod to plank and 3 beams to lay.
> 3   Next, the third span belongs again to the bishop, and (there are) 2½ rods to plank and 3 beams to lay. * * *
> 4   Next, the fourth span is the king's, and (there are) 3½ rods to plank and 3 beams to lay. * * *
> 5   Next, the fifth span is the archbishop's, * * * and (there are) 4 rods to plank and 3 beams to lay.
> 6   Next, the sixth span is for Hollingbourne and all the district, and (there are) 4 rods to plank and 3 beams to lay.
> 7-8   Next, the seventh and eighth spans are for the Hoo people's land to construct, and (there are) 4½ rods to plank and 6 beams to lay.
> 9   Next, the ninth span is the archbishop's, that is the landspan at the west end, * * * and (there are) 4 rods to plank and 3 beams to lay.

NOTES

1   The structure seems to have been more or less completely rebuilt between about 1490 and 1530 (Britnell 1994, pp. 73-5). After that, the most visible change that occurred was in 1821-4, when two of the spans were removed and replaced with one double-sized arch (Ormrod 1994, pp. 217-8).

2   The feud between the S. E. R. and the L. C. & D. is a long story, recounted briefly by White (1961), in detail by Gray (1984, 1990).

3   The superstructure of the nineteenth-century roadbridge was entirely rebuilt in 1911-14. At about the same time, in 1910-11, the L. C. & D. line was diverted onto the S. E. R. bridge, and the earlier railway bridge became redundant. It lay derelict for many years, till finally the piers were adapted to carry a new roadway for eastbound traffic in the 1960s.

4   In time this cartulary came to form part of the composite volume known to historians as the 'Textus Roffensis'; but it was, originally, a distinct piece of work. The 'Textus' − Strood, Rochester upon Medway Studies Centre, DRc/R1 − is available in facsimile (Sawyer 1957-62) and on microfilm (Harvester Press 1987).

5   I discussed some of these vernacular documents in a previous paper (Flight 1996). In the case of the bridgework text, the Latin version is placed first, and Brooks (1994, p. 366) may be right to suggest that this ordering reflects the compiler's 'perception of the status of the two languages'. But the point is doubtful, because in both the other cases the English version has precedence. Four English texts appear in the cartulary without an accompanying translation: Campbell 1973, nos. 36-7, plus the two printed by Pelteret (1986, p. 493, from fol. 162r-v).

6   If they had been numbered by the original scribe, the leaves of quire VI would have been fols. 41-49; but in fact the cartulary was not foliated till much later, after it had been bound up in tandem with another manuscript, which consists of 118 leaves. The first leaf of the cartulary, therefore, is fol. 119.

7   There are several other places in the cartulary where something similar has happened; one such instance is cited below (note 14).

8   The word *de* before *gisleardes* was inserted by the later scribe. It is written in ligature − with the *e* riding on the back of the *d* − and that is one of the tricks which distinguish his hand from that of the main scribe (and which also prove it to be considerably later). Brooks's note (1994, p. 365, note u) overlooks this point.

9   But the ligatured *de* in line 2 and the ugly ampersand at the end of line 6 are characteristic of the later scribe.

10   In one respect, however, he seems to have thought himself capable of improving on his exemplar. The spelling *yo* (corresponding to West Saxon *eo*) occurs fairly consistently in the portion of the text written by the main scribe (*syo*, *þryo*, *syoxte*, *syoueþe*, *flyote*), but it does not occur at all in the rewritten portion. Here we find instead the spellings *eo* and *io*, which, conversely, do not occur in the second portion of the text. It looks as if this later scribe took a dislike to the spelling *yo* and insisted on changing it into something else.

11   After examining the original, I am satisfied that Robertson (1939, p. 108, note 10) was right: this is a blank, not an erasure. Brooks (1994) describes the facts correctly in one place (p. 17, note 33), incorrectly in another (p. 363, note c). The distinction does make a difference. If this were an erasure, it would mean that the names were removed from the list after this page was recopied; because it is a blank (imitating a preexisting erasure) it means that the names were removed before that happened.

12   The list of names has been reorganized in this document, so we cannot be sure that this was the original order.

13 Loose and Linton belonged to the monks of Christ Church. Perhaps it was they who thought of asking for the bridgework text to be appropriately amended.

14 The same layout was used for a list of the parish churches in the diocese of Rochester (fols. 220v-222r). Here too the original scribe anticipated that this list would need to be consulted; here too he was evidently right. One leaf has been excised (between fols. 220 and 221) and the text from it recopied onto the verso of the preceding leaf, which was conveniently blank; besides, there are several erasures and alterations in the original portion of the list.

15 Nor do we know what became of the two leaves excised from the cartulary: they may perhaps have been kept.

16 One odd feature of the Latin version is its treatment of the phrase *and of ufanhylle* occurring in the list of places liable for work on the fourth segment. At first this was translated as *et de supermontaneis*, 'and from the hilltop people'. Eventually someone realized that these words referred to a place – the place called Ovenhill or Overhill – not to a group of people, and the phrase *et de ufenhylle* was incorporated into the text. However, instead of being substituted for the existing phrase, this new phrase was interpolated at a point further on, and the text thus came to read *et de supermontaneis, ... et de ufenhylle*. In *Privilegia*, the new phrase is written in the margin, with the intended point of insertion clearly marked. If this marginal addition had been written by the scribe who wrote the rest of this page, as is stated to be the case by Brooks (1994, p. 365, note p), we might fairly infer that this quirk in the text originated here, and that other copies, because they suffer from the same quirk, must therefore all derive from *Privilegia*. But that inference seems unsafe to me, because the initial condition is not met: the hand which wrote these words in the margin was (in my judgement) definitely not the same hand which wrote the rest of this page.

17 Sooner or later, the Exchequer apparently decided that it would be useful to have a copy of this document on file. In 1391, when the builders of the new bridge submitted their proposals for its future maintenance, they attached a copy of the bridgework text (*Rotuli parliamentorum*, vol. 3, p. 289); and their copy carries the title 'Domesday for the bridge of Rochester according to the Exchequer (*selonc leschequer*)' (Britnell 1994, p. 50, note 50; cf. Brooks 1994, p. 364, note a). However, it does not seem to be possible to identify an Exchequer version of the text, recognizably different from the Rochester version.

18 One fourteenth-century document (Public Record Office, Exchequer Accounts, E 101/510/16) needs to be mentioned only to be discounted. It appears in the published catalogue as 'Particulars of the account of the citizens of Rochester of the profits of Rochester ferry' (*Lists and indexes*, vol. 35, p. 310). Though the document is in bad condition, and very difficult to read, I can decipher enough to see that it refers, not to a ferry, but to a fair (*feria*) held in the city on St Dunstan's day. The right to hold a three-day fair – beginning on the day before and ending on the day after the feast of St Dunstan (19 May) – was one of the privileges granted or confirmed to the citizens in the fifteenth century (*Calendar of charter rolls 1427-1516*, pp. 63-4, 179).

19 *Calendar of fine rolls 1337-47*, p. 146; *Calendar of patent rolls 1336-40*, p. 323; PRO, Exchequer Accounts, E 101/507/20 (Burtt 1866, p. 117; Becker 1930, p. 4), with a matching entry

on the pipe roll (and on the chancellor's roll); Coram Rege roll, Easter 1340 (Flower 1915, pp. 204-8).

20 Two surviving copies are cited by Brooks (1994, p. 367), both originating in Canterbury, both dating from the first half of the fourteenth century, the second seemingly copied from the first (p. 369, notes y, a2).

21 On the evidence of the information it gives regarding Wouldham (below, note 24).

22 Some of the places named did not in fact belong to Eyhorne hundred. Most notably, Boxley and Detling were in Maidstone hundred, and for Boxley at least that appears to have been true as far back as the 1080s. Ward (1934, pp. 19-20) discussed this anomaly, but I doubt whether his proposed explanation has any particular cogency.

23 Several of the assessments were disputed. For example, the men of Boxley are reported to be answerable for 7½ sulungs, 'but they do not agree to (*contradicunt*) the half sulung'. This makes it clear, as Brooks points out, that the report was the product of some official inquiry. Some readers may like to be reminded that a sulung was a measure of arable land, peculiar to Kent, denoting the area which could in theory be ploughed by one team of oxen (Witney 1992). A yoke was a fraction of a sulung, usually one quarter (implying that the team would normally consist of eight oxen), but not invariably so. In the hundred of Hoo, for instance, around 1200, there were six yokes in a sulung (Kemp 1986, pp. 323-4). Like hides elsewhere, sulungs and yokes were used for the allocation of taxes. Around the mid twelfth century, there were reckoned to be 1058 taxable sulungs (plus a fraction) in the county as a whole.

24 With regard to Wouldham (assessed at 3 sulungs in all), it is stated explicitly that the burden should be shared 'with Robert Biset and his partners and with Robert Neve' (*cum Roberto Biset et sociis suis et cum Roberto Neve*). This refers to the two holdings (assessed at 1 sulung and ½ sulung respectively) which had been carved out of the manor of Wouldham for the bishop's knights (Thorpe 1788, p. 2); the former was known as Little Wouldham. Tenants named Robert Biset and Robert le Neve occur together in documents dating from about 1230 (e.g. a writ printed by Robinson 1933, p. 83).

25 In other words, I suggest that the men of Aylesford tried appealing to the same principle known to have been vainly invoked by the men of Eyhorne: that nobody ought to be made to pay for mending more than one bridge (below, p. 19). If that was their case, they were equally unsuccessful. Though omitted here, they were back on the list in 1343 (Appendix 2, no. 5).

26 Solutions are easy to think up: the difficulty lies in deciding which is best (i.e. most likely to be true). It is conceivable, for instance, that the names erased from *Privilegia* survived in one or both of the (hypothetical) single sheets. Assuming that to be true, we could imagine various ways of arriving at the conflated version of the text which lies behind the Hollingbourne memorandum, without needing to postulate the existence of any additional copies.

27 'Collected and written (for the most part) in the yeare 1570 ... and nowe increased by the addition of some things which the Authour him selfe hath obserued since that time' (Lambarde 1576, titlepage). Since Lambarde did not see the 'Textus Roffensis' till 1573, the documents he printed from that source,

including the two versions of the bridgework text, must have been among the additions which he made at the last minute, before letting his manuscript be sent to the printer. For these documents we need to consult the original edition of Lambarde's book; for general purposes, however, the most useful edition is the second, 'increased and altered after the Authors owne last Copie', published in 1596. Subsequent editions are not to be relied on.

28 It is, indeed, very tempting to emend some of the mistakes in this portion of the text; and Lambarde may even have been justified in thinking that he had a better grasp of Old English grammar and spelling than the scribe who recopied this page. Nevertheless, the temptation has to be resisted, for two good reasons. First, once one starts emending, it is not clear where to stop. Second, it is not clear what one is emending to. Is the emendation supposed to restore the text to what was written by the main scribe? or to what appeared in his exemplar? or to what was in the mind of the original author? Since there is no point is asking unanswerable questions, we had better not put ourselves into a position where such questions have to be asked.

29 The misprint occurs in paragraph 6. The text is given as *7 iiii. sylla to leccenne*; the translation reads *and foure plates to laye* (Lambarde 1576, p. 310). I have seen a copy of the first edition (the copy in the Library of Congress, Washington, D.C.) with the variant reading *and three plates to laye*. From the unevenness of the type, it looks as if *three* was a correction; but the uncorrected reading *foure* was the one which persisted into the second edition, and so into every other printed version of the text – till Robertson's (see below). In the Latin version the numeral appears correctly: *& 3. suliuas supponere* (p. 312).

30 Nicholas Wotton, dean of Canterbury, was a member of the royal commission set up in 1561 to find out what arrangements were supposed to exist for maintaining Rochester bridge, and to suggest how they might be made more effective (Gibson 1994, pp. 119-26); a worried letter written to Wotton by another member of the commission in December 1564 (Gibson 1994, p. 125) suggests that the Hollingbourne memorandum had only just been discovered. Dr Wotton died in 1567. His nephew John Wotton was a close friend of Lambarde's; he supervised the printing of the *Perambulation*.

31 Apparently neither of the copies cited by Brooks was the source of Wotton's transcript (Brooks 1994, p. 369, note a2).

32 Later on, in 1585, Lambarde became a member of the corporation responsible for managing the bridge, and he renewed the search for documentation. A collection of transcripts – 'A Kalendar of the Evidences of Rochester bridge hitherto discovered & copyed into the blacke lidgier booke of the said Bridge' – was put together in 1595 (Gibson 1994, p. 143). I have not consulted this.

33 Harris (1719, pp. 259-61) used one of the seventeenth-century editions of Lambarde's book; Hearne (1720, pp. 379-83) used the second edition. Hasted did not reprint the text: more usefully, he provided his readers with an annotated translation of the Latin version (Hasted 1782, p. 16, omitted from the second edition, where the whole account of the bridge is drastically shortened).

34 Birch inherited two of Lambarde's errors, including the misprinted numeral. In addition, a few new errors crept into the text.

35 There are three small mistakes (*Hroucæstre*, p. 106, line 24; *gebyrað*, p. 108, line 2; *Ægelesforda*, line 8) and one questionable reading (*Cærstane*, line 12). Text, translation and notes are all reproduced identically in the second edition (Robertson 1956). Brooks (1994, pp. 362-4) has printed the document again, not very accurately. His text seems to be a copy of Robertson's, with which it shares two errors; it also has several errors of its own.

36 To judge from the examples quoted by the *New English Dictionary* (Murray 1909) – which is the source of the article in the *Oxford English Dictionary* – 'pere' or 'peere' was the normal spelling until the mid 1600s. After that, people mostly wrote 'peer', until about the mid 1700s, when the modern spelling 'pier' became canonical. The shift from 'pere' to 'peer' was part of a general overhaul of English spelling (reflected, for instance, in the 1663 edition of the works of Shakespeare). The shift from 'peer' to 'pier' is anomalous; I do not know whether any plausible explanation can be suggested for it, unless perhaps it reflects some influence from French.

37 Away from Rochester, the earliest examples quoted by the *New English Dictionary* come from the late fourteenth-century translation (ed. Herrtage 1879) of a French romance, called *Sir Ferumbras*, which happens to contain a description of a bridge. Here the word *per* occurs twice, two lines apart. From the context, and from the parallel French, it seems clear in the first instance that *per* means 'arch' ('Sixty *pers* ... that are great and round') and in the second that it means 'pier' ('Upon each *per* there stands a tower'). The corresponding words in the French text are *ars*, 'arches', and *piler*, 'pillar', respectively. It is strange to find a word used in contrary senses so close together; but the author was writing a poem, not an engineering manual, and perhaps he did not stop to think that a tower would have to be built on top of a pier, rather than at the centre of a span.

38 According to Brooks (1994, p. 364) the word is of 'variable gender'; but I think that the variation exists only in the later scribe's spelling. In the portion written by the main scribe, the nominative is always *syo per*, which has to be feminine. The accusative *þa peran* was construed as plural by Robertson (1939, p. 106); but if feminine it could equally well be singular, and that is what the context requires.

39 There is a Latin word *pera*, borrowed from Greek, which occurs, for example, in the Vulgate translation of the Bible (Luke 9:3, 10:4); but this *pera* means 'satchel, scrip', the sort of bag which a traveller carries with him. Though words can change their meanings in some very peculiar ways, it is hard to imagine how a word meaning 'bag' could come to mean 'part of a bridge'.

40 Manning to Gough, dd. Godalming, 18 September 1783 (printed by Nichols 1831, p. 304, note).

41 Flight (1996, p. 137, note 23) will, I hope, be the last person to mistranslate the word. Perhaps it is permissible for me to say that I arrived at the right conclusion independently, before seeing Manning's letter. But I am mortified to think how long it took me to reach a point which somebody else had reached, more than two hundred years sooner, seemingly without any effort.

42 In the Latin version the eastern *landper* is called *prima pera de terra*, which means, I suppose, 'the first span from the land'.

43 Appendix 2, no. 5, the report of an inquiry held at Rochester in 1343. The places liable for work on the first segment of the bridge are stated to be responsible for 'the wharf and the woodwork and earthwork up to the second *pera* (*usque ad secundam peram*), so that part is called the first *pera* of the bridge (*et sic vocatur illa parcella prima pera pontis predicti*)'. Because of the wharf, span 1 was a special case (below, p. 42); but this does not alter the fact that some effort was being made to clarify the meaning of the word *pera*. Brooks seems to overlook the importance of this passage, which — from his point of view — would surely prove that 'reconstruction A' should be preferred (Brooks 1994, fig. 4).

44 He did not mean to say that the bridge consisted *either* of nine arches (implying ten piers) *or else* of nine piers (implying eight arches), but that he did not know which. For him, the words 'arche' and 'pere' were equivalent. By putting 'Arches' first, he may be implying that he expects his readers to be more familiar with this word; but he does not expect them to boggle at the other. (It has to be said, however, that he seems to be contradicting himself on the next page, where he suggests that *pera* may be derived from *petra*, meaning 'rock'.) The equation of 'pere' and 'arche' is also implied by a schedule drawn up in 1587 (Gibson 1994, p. 151), when the wardens were making a vain attempt to resuscitate the arrangements relating to the maintenance of the old bridge.

45 What the dictionaries ought to say, it seems, is something to this effect: **pier** (1) *per, pere, peere*, 'arch, opening, span of a bridge', obsolete; (2) *pere, peere, peer, pier*, 'structure supporting a bridge'. The first sense would be illustrated by the bridgework text, by one of the lines from *Sir Ferumbras* (above, note 37), and by Lambarde's remark equating 'arch' and 'pere'. Examples of the second sense would begin with the other line from *Sir Ferumbras*; and Manning's remark contrasting this sense with the obsolete sense 1 might also be cited here.

2

Place-names

The geography of the bridgework text will need to be discussed at some length, not so much for its own sake, but rather because it is through a study of the place-names that we can gain some idea of how the text evolved, over time, into the form in which it is known to us. With only a few exceptions, the place-names had been identified successfully, before 1731, by the antiquary John Thorpe.[1] By then, places lying more than seven miles from the bridge (or, more precisely, lying in a parish which lay more than seven miles from the bridge) had long since been released from any obligation to it.[2] Within a seven-mile radius, therefore, the places which had been liable in the fourteenth century were still theoretically liable four hundred years later, and Thorpe's identifications ought to be secure; but outside that circle there was no continuity, and the identifications proposed by Thorpe are of a more conjectural kind.

There is one blind alley which I do not propose to explore. Ward (1934) had the idea that the catchment area for bridgework at Rochester might once have been exactly congruent with the district which in Domesday Book is called the *lest* of Aylesford. On the surface at least, this theory is manifestly false, both positively and negatively. Some of the places named in the text did not belong to the lathe of Aylesford; many places which did belong are not named in the text. That much is certain. Nevertheless, if there were some strong presumption in favour of Ward's theory, we might think that we ought to make it our task to explain away all the anomalies which seem to contradict it. That is what Ward set himself to do, with some degree of success; and that is what Brooks has done again just recently (1992, pp. 14-15; 1994, pp. 26-30). But I do not see any presumption in favour of Ward's theory, nor any point in denying the obvious fact that it is − at best − only very roughly true.[3] There is no hint in the text that the bridge as a whole was superintended by any single entity. On the contrary, we might think that it was precisely the lack of such an entity − larger than a hundred but smaller than the whole shire − which made it necessary for these seemingly ad hoc arrangements to be worked out.

Ideally, we would expect the catchment area for one bridge to be determined by the catchment areas for neighbouring bridges, through some process of mutual adjustment (with the aim of ensuring that every bridge could command sufficient labour but that nobody had to do more than a fair share or travel excessively far).[4] The difficulty is, of course, that we do not have any clear idea what other bridges existed, or what places were responsible for repairing them; so for us the Rochester text exists in a vacuum.[5] Nevertheless, when we find four places being removed from the Rochester list during the twelfth century (above, p. 3), we are not to infer that they were being exempted from bridgework altogether: the presumption is rather that they had been made responsible for some other bridge.

For five of the spans, the text gives us a detailed list of the places which had to contribute. To some extent, these lists were fluid, open to alteration as conditions changed. Some of these alterations are visible to us, as erasures or blanks in *Privilegia*, and in the Hollingbourne memorandum too (Brooks 1994, pp. 368-9, notes v, y, a2). It is likely enough that other such alterations were made from time to time, in circumstances which meant that they left no visible traces. Apart from piecemeal changes of this kind, there is reason to think that these parts of the text underwent some drastic revision on two occasions at least. In other words, the text as we have it seems to a palimpsest of three different versions. To understand this, we need to work backwards through time, beginning with the latest − i.e. the third − layer of text.

Layer 3

As far as this layer is concerned, the essential facts have already been explained by Brooks (1994, p. 18). It is more or less certain that the paragraphs relating to the bishop's two spans (1 and 3) were modified some time after the 1120s, probably around the beginning of the thirteenth century. In contrast with the archbishop's spans, where most of the places named never belonged to Canterbury, the places named in connection with the bishop's spans (Fig. 3)

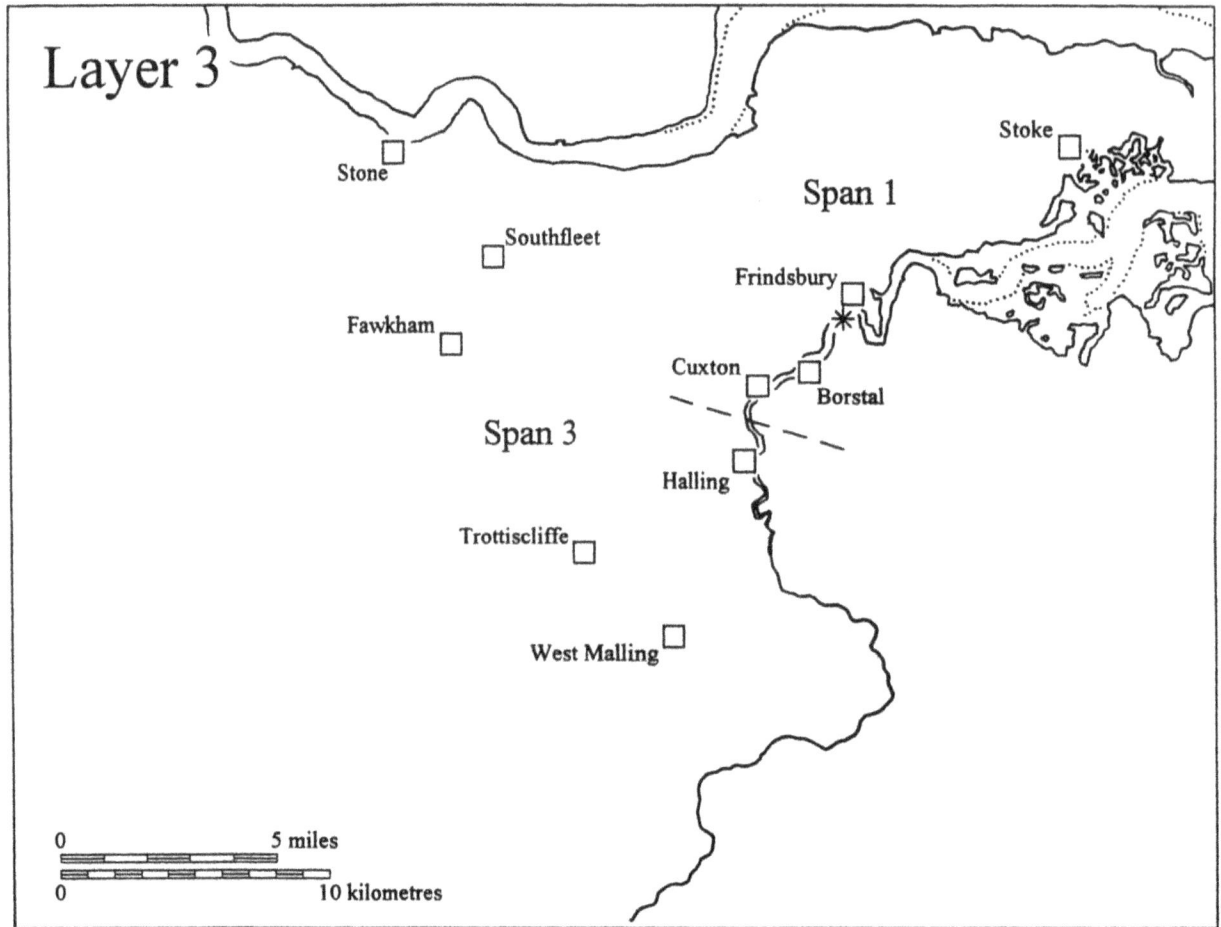

Fig. 3. Places named in Layer 3 (not shown: *Pinindene*).

were all the property of the church of Rochester.[6] From the 1080s onwards, some belonged to the bishop, some to the monks.[7] In *Privilegia*, the leaf which contained the first few paragraphs of the Latin text has been replaced, and so has the leaf which contained the first few paragraphs of the English text (above, p. 2). The only assignable reason why this might have been done is so that modifications could be made in paragraphs 1 and 3.

Such changes could not have been made surreptitiously. For a start, I suppose, the king would have had to be consulted. More than that, I imagine that the bishop would have had to negotiate with his tenants. We can understand why he might have been unhappy with an arrangement which meant that he was being held answerable for the conduct of people over whom he had no leverage. From his point of view, it would obviously be better if all the money (in lieu of labour) was supplied by his own tenants, or by the monks' tenants (not quite the same thing, but close). Some places – places which had succeeded in causing more trouble than they were worth – were presumably allowed to shed their

responsibility for the bridge; and the load was transferred to the bishop's and the monks' own manors. In return for agreeing to this, however, their tenants would have had to be compensated somehow, through a downward adjustment of the other rents and services they owed.[8]

The intention may have been that the number of sulungs liable for spans 1 and 3 should be at least roughly equal, but it is not clear how nearly this result was achieved. The figures from Domesday Book cited by Brooks (1992, p. 18) are the assessments said to have applied 'in the time of king Eadward', and these are plainly not the most relevant figures. The assessments reported to be current 'now', i.e. in the 1080s, add up to 13·5 sulungs for pan 1 and 16 sulungs for span 3 (not counting *Pinindene*). But the figures we really want, of course, are the assessments which applied in about 1200, when this arrangement was worked out. The only numbers I can quote which are of about the right date are the assessments recorded by early thirteenth-century Rochester sources for the manors belonging to the monks;[9] and these figures, without exception, are different from the figures reported for the 1080s. In short, we know enough to see that we cannot rely on the evidence of Domesday Book for deciding whether the arrangement was equitable, but not enough to answer the question in any other way. All the same, so far as we can compare these two spans with other parts of the bridge – with spans 5 and 9, for instance, for each of which the cost was distributed over more than 40 sulungs in the 1080s (below, p. 15) – it looks as if the burden which fell on the bishop's tenants was disproportionately heavy.

From the dating of the script of the two rewritten pages, it seems very likely that the bishop who initiated these changes was bishop Gilbert (1185-1214), who, from other evidence, is known to have been an energetic reformer – too energetic, in the opinion of some. In fact, he is also known to have taken an interest in the bridge (Appendix 2, nos. 2-3). It was Gilbert, I suppose, who overhauled the arrangements relating to spans 1 and 3, and who made sure that copies of the bridgework text were suitably amended. In this – unluckily for us – he was wholly successful: the derivative texts are all in agreement with the revised version of paragraphs 1 and 3. Thus we have no clear indication what the previous arrangements might have been.

But of course it is not be thought that the new arrangement was new in every respect, and that none of the places named here had been liable for bridgework before. On the contrary, by analogy with the paragraphs concerning the archbishop's spans, the preexisting lists are likely to have each begun with one or two places belonging to the church of Rochester. In light of that, it might be thought significant, for instance, that the spelling *Borcsteall*, for the first place in paragraph 1, has a very old-fashioned look to it. It is true that a thirteenth-century scribe, left to his own devices, would normally have written *Borstalle* or something similar;[10] but in this context, I think, he might have preferred to affect a suitably antique spelling, or what he believed to be such. If that is agreed to be possible, the evidence of spelling will not by itself be enough to prove that a name was retained from some earlier version of the list.

The inclusion of Borstal is significant, more directly, because it proves straight away that in layer 3 the names were intended to refer to manors, not parishes. There was no parish of Borstal. Around 1200 (i.e. around the time when this list achieved its final

form), the manor of Borstal was part of the parish of St Margaret;[11] and that parish included three other manors – Nashenden, Upper Delce, Lower Delce – all of which are named in Domesday Book,[12] but all of which are absent (perhaps we might say conspicuously absent) from the bridgework text. Similarly, the manor of Stoke was not coincident with the parish of Stoke, part of which had been a separate holding since before 1066.[13] The tenants of the other Stoke would not have taken kindly to the idea that they should share the burden of repairing the bishop's span. Examples could be cited elsewhere too;[14] but there is no need to emphasize an obvious fact. To put it briefly, though manors and parishes often shared a name, very often they differed in extent; and that fact left scope for disagreement and dispute at the time, not to speak of the difficulty which it causes for us.[15]

Layer 2

The lists which I take to belong to layer 2 are those occurring in paragraphs 5 and 9, i.e. in the paragraphs relating to the archbishop's spans. These lists semble one another, and diverge from the other three,[16] in two small but significant respects. First, the other lists use the preposition *of*, meaning 'from': the wording runs *of X and of Y and of Z ...* . But the lists in paragraphs 5 and 9 are differently worded, *to X and to Y and to Z ...* . Second, in these two cases the list occurs in the middle of the paragraph, not at the end – before the clause relating to the planks and beams, not after it. On the evidence of these discrepancies, I think we can feel fairly sure that paragraphs 5 and 9 have also undergone revision.

Except that it must have happened before the 1120s (when the resulting version of the text was copied into *Privilegia*), this revision is difficult to date. Since most of the places named here did not belong to the church of Canterbury, the fact that some of them did cannot be expected to tell us anything about the dating; nor can the fact that some were the property of the church of Rochester.[17]

Since the compiler of the cartulary included this document in the booklet devoted to pre-conquest documents, he seems to have thought that it dated from that period. For him, more precisely, the break did not come with the battle of Hastings, or with the coronation of Willelm I. It came with the arrival of Lanfranc, the archbishop who took the church of Rochester under his wing, rebuilding it totally and manning it with monks; and Lanfranc did not appear

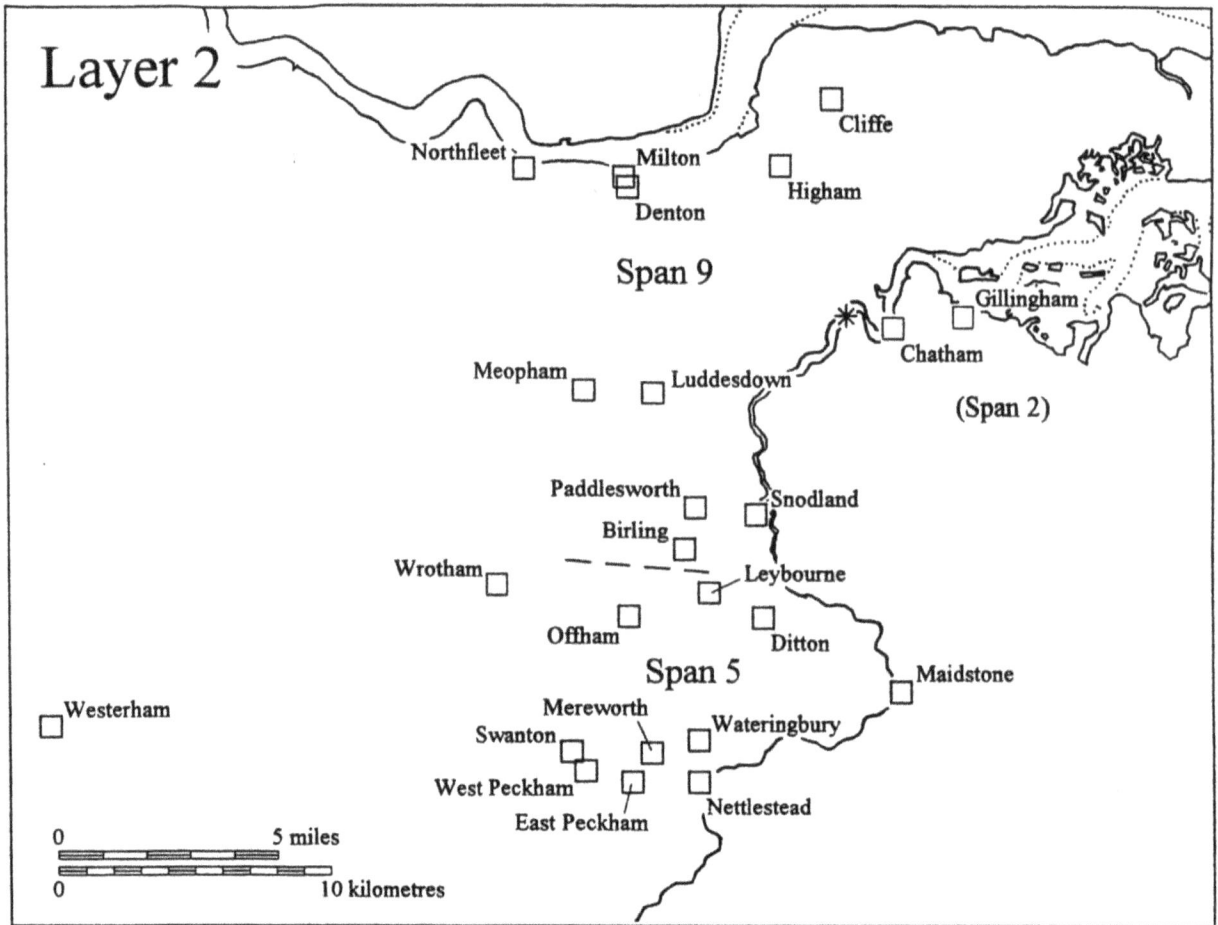

Fig. 4. Places named in Layer 2 (not shown: *Hæselholt*).

on the scene until 1070. The bridgework text, we may gather, was thought to be earlier than that. Furthermore, under the new arrangements instituted by Lanfranc the bishop of Rochester became the archbishop's coadjutor, and he also became his tenant: from the 1070s onwards, any reorganization initiated by the archbishop would be expected to cover the bishop's spans in addition to his own. Because it did not do that, the change which resulted in layer 2 is likely to have occurred previously, at a time when the bishop of Rochester was an independent agent, to more or less the same degree as any other bishop. On that evidence, I think we can safely conclude that layer 2 is earlier than 1070.

Unlike the list in paragraph 4 (see below), which allows us a glimpse of a very undomesdaylike landscape, the situation reflected in these two paragraphs (Fig. 4) is largely the same as the situation reported in the 1080s. With only two exceptions – *Hæselholt* and *Swanatun* – all the places named in layer 2 are places which occur in Domesday Book.[18] More specifically, the fact that Cliffe is called 'his Cliffe' implies that the archbishop did not possess the whole

place; and in Domesday Book, sure enough, a small part of Cliffe is listed as a separate holding (fol. 9ra). Again, the text makes a point of saying 'the two Peckhams', so as not to leave room for doubt; and in Domesday Book we find two Peckhams recorded (fols. 4vb, 7va-b). Both at Cliffe and at Peckham the division had existed already 'in the time of king Eadward', i.e. before 1066. On the other hand, the text does *not* say 'the two Wateringburys' or 'the two Offhams', though these places too were both subdivided 'in the time of king Eadward' and remained so twenty years later.[19] In a few details, therefore, the landscape reflected in layer 2 may perhaps have been different from – and if so presumably earlier than – the landscape existing in the 1060s.

As well as telling us the names, Domesday Book reports the number of sulungs for which each place was answerable; it also reports whether the assessment had changed between 1066 and 1086. It may be possible to read some chronological significance into these data. By adding up the figures reported there for the places named in paragraphs 5 and 9, we arrive at the totals given in Table 1.[20] Though the data are incomplete, and quite possibly flawed, it is tempting to suppose that the number of sulungs was originally intended to be − as nearly as possible − the same for both spans. Since many of the assessments are small (two sulungs or less), it would not be difficult to achieve an almost equal partition, if that were the objective. By the 1080s, through time and chance, the division of labour had become distinctly unequal; but it seems to have been much more nearly equal in the 1060s.[21] By this argument, such as it is, layer 2 in its original (perfectly equitable) form would date from before 1066, but perhaps not long before.

Date	1066	1086	1340
span 5	44	43.25	34.5
span 9	43.375	34.875	n.d.

Table 1. Total numbers of sulungs
answerable for spans 5 and 9

Neither of these arguments is strong, but they are at least consistent with one another, and with a third argument which seems to be relevant here. In the text as a whole, some features of the spelling have been thought to suggest that it passed through the hands of an early or mid eleventh-century scribe.[22] Here we are dealing with microscopic details, and much depends on the reliability of the copyists concerned in the subsequent transmission of the text. The main scribe of *Privilegia* can certainly be trusted: he has a well-deserved reputation for honesty and accuracy. In some cases it is possible to compare his copy with the exemplar from which he worked, and it thus becomes clear that he was doing his best to copy letter for letter, and was nearly always successful in doing so. He was comfortable with the vernacular as well as with Latin; in fact, he has two styles of script, and switches smoothly from one to the other, as the language changes. The later scribe is not somebody we know, and there are some fairly clear indications that he was disconcerted by the strangeness of the language (above, p. 2). His spellings cannot be so safely assumed to reproduce those of his exemplar.

At first sight, the most striking fact about the spelling is its variability. The word *lecgan* is spelt in four different ways (but always with *cc* for *cg*), the word *þilian* in six. Some of this inconsistency may be due to the later scribe; but most of it is not. Even in the stretch of text copied by the main scribe there

are three different spellings for *lecgan* and four for *þilian*. Thus it would seem that both these scribes (the main scribe perhaps more successfully) were copying letter for letter, controlling the impulse to regularize or modernize the spelling. They preserved the variation: they did not create it. Further back in time, this text had been handled by at least one scribe with very relaxed ideas about orthography − a scribe who seems to have enjoyed inventing different ways of spelling the same word. In assessing the evidence of spelling, therefore, these and similar reservations have to be borne in mind.

The name Rochester happens to be a rather good reflector of the shifts in pronunciation and spelling which were under way during the eleventh century. The 'classical' tenth-century spelling was (for the oblique cases) *Hrofesceastre*; the usual twelfth-century spelling was *Rouecestre*.[23] Two documents which I take to have been drawn up in the 990s, by a scribe working for the bishop (Flight 1996), both adhere to the 'classical' spelling, though in other documents of around the same date the first *s* tends to vanish. The only surviving document (Pelteret 1986, p. 493, from *Privilegia*, fol. 162v) drawn up in Rochester in the time of bishop Siward (1058-1074?) has the spelling *Hrouecæstre*, exactly the same as in the (rewritten portion of the) bridgework text.

From these admittedly meagre indications, I conclude that the document which eventually came to be copied into *Privilegia* is most likely to have been written circa 1040-70, and that layer 2 became part of the text at that time. Given that dating, the archbishop responsible for this revision of the text would presumably have been either Eadsige (1038-1050) or Stigand (1052-1070); perhaps the former might be thought the likelier.

There are two puzzles associated with layer 2. First, at the end of the list of place-names in paragraph 9 we find the phrase *and ealla þa dænewaru*. The Latin version takes *dæne-* to signify 'valley': 'and from all those men who dwell in that valley (*qui manent in illa ualle*)'. But it is hard to imagine what that might mean, or even what it might have been thought to mean by the author of the Latin version. In fact, as Brooks (1994, p. 18, note 35) points out, the people intended seem sure to have been the inhabitants of the denns, the settlements in the Weald where herds of pigs were kept: the spelling *dænn* (for *denn*) is attested in Kentish documents.[24] This emendation improves the sense considerably, and I think it must be right. But that is not the only difficulty. The

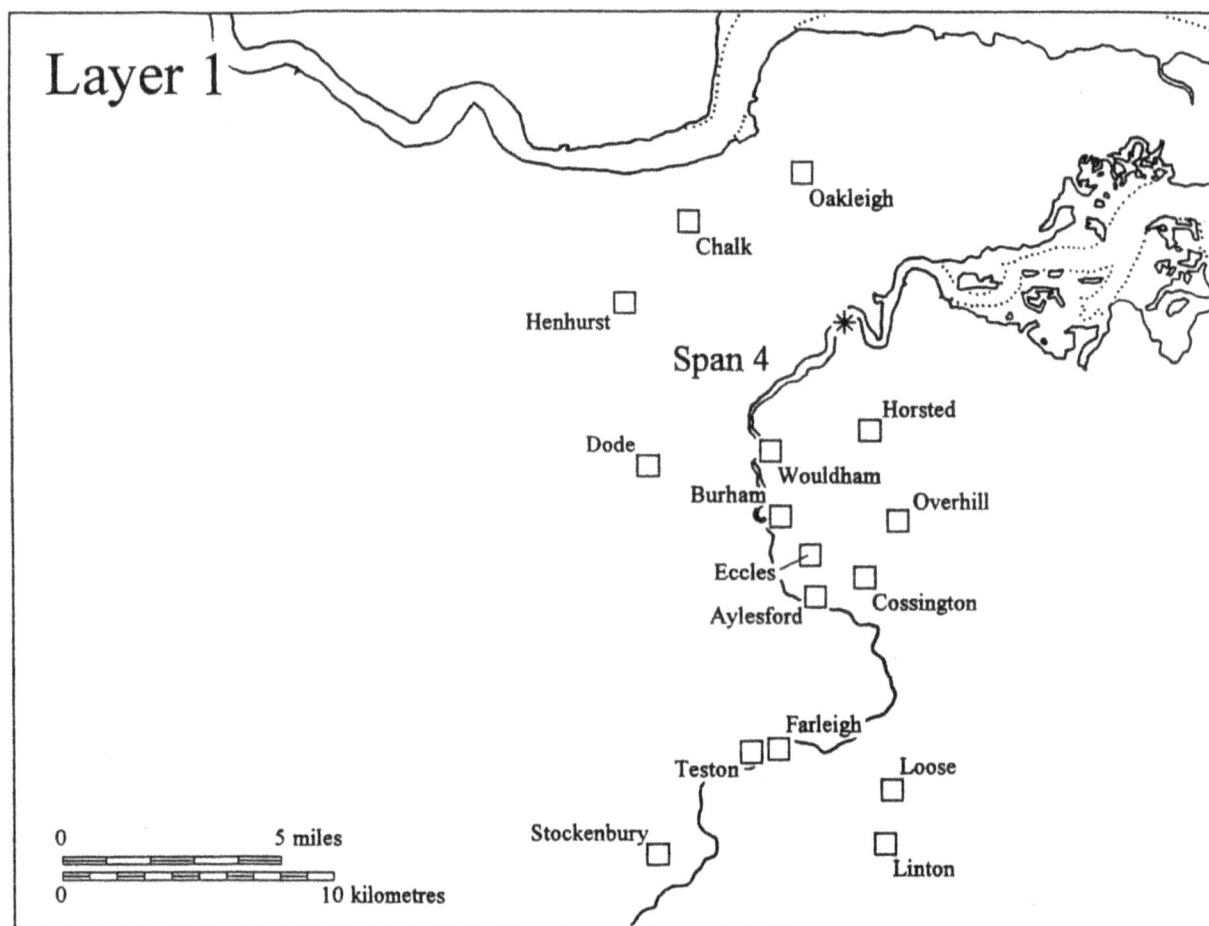

Fig. 5. Places named in Layer 1 (not shown: 'the narrow land',
Gisleardesland, Lichebundelonde, Ædun).

syntax is not coherent: these words are not properly connected with the preceding list.[25] I suggest that they may be a fragment of a lost sentence − 'and all the people of the denns (are to do such and such)' − surviving from an earlier version of the text, mistakenly attached to the end of this list of place-names.

Second, it seems possible that span 2 was also, at some stage, under the archbishop's supervision. Paragraph 2, as written by the later scribe, says *Þanne seo oðer per gebyraþ to Gyllingeham and to Cætham*, 'Next the second span belongs to Gillingham and Chatham', followed by the usual specifications relating to planks and beams. Since Gillingham was the archbishop's property, this could be read as a list constructed in exactly the same way as the lists occurring in paragraphs 5 and 9 (i.e. headed by one of the archbishop's manors, concatenated by the words *and to*, placed in the middle of the paragraph), differing only in being very much shorter. It is conceivable, therefore, that at some stage what this paragraph said was *Þonne syo oðer per gebyraþ* [*þam arcebiscope*], 'Next the second

span belongs [to the archbishop]', and that the bracketed words were lost − omitted by accident or (more probably) deleted on purpose − at some point in the transmission of the text.

Layer 1

The only list which remains unaccounted for is the list of places responsible − under the king − for repairing the fourth span; and what we find here (Fig. 5) is a much more surprising collection of names than the domesdaylike collections occurring in layers 2 and 3.

The list is headed by Aylesford, which, in the late eleventh century, was one of the king's own possessions, and had probably always been so (whatever 'always' may mean);[26] presumably it was managed by a reeve, a *tungerefa*, answerable to the king. Next there is the mention of a 'lathe' − a lathe of which Aylesford was, in some sense, the focal point: we are told that the labour is to come not only 'from

16

Aylesford' but also 'from all the lathe that lies to it'.[27] This means, I suppose, that the reeve of Aylesford had some sphere of responsibility extending beyond the lands which came directly under his management.

If we classify the other names on our own terms, i.e. according to how and how much we know about them, we can sort them into three groups.[28] Group A consists of all the names known to us from Domesday Book. Not counting Aylesford, ten fall into this category: Oakleigh, Wouldham, Burham, Eccles,[29] Stockenbury, Farleigh,[30] Teston, Chalk, Henhurst, and *Hathdune*.[31] The identifications are not all equally definite, but I do not think that any of them are seriously in doubt. Group B consists of the names not recorded in Domesday Book but known from other sources. There are six such names: Overhill, Cossington,[32] Dode,[33] Loose, Linton,[34] and Horsted. The same cautionary comment which applies to the first ten names applies to these names too. Group C consists of three names which are otherwise quite unknown: 'the narrow land', 'Gislheard's land', and one name which seems to have been so badly mangled (by copyists to whom it meant nothing) that we cannot be sure of much beyond '......d's land'.[35]

Layer	1	2	3	Totals
Group A	11	21	10	42
Group B	6	2	1	9
Group C	3	0	0	3
Totals	20	23	11	54

Table 2. Classification of the place-names
in layers 1-3

The same classification applied to the other layers of text will give us the rest of the figures in Table 2.[36] By this reckoning, the domesdaylike layers 2 and 3 are not appreciably different from one another, even though probably more than a century apart. Layer 1, however, is distinctly different from both. Group A accounts for more than nine-tenths of the names in layers 2-3, but for not much more than half of the names in layer 1. Furthermore, of the names erased from *Privilegia*, three belong to groups B or C, only one to group A; so the effect of these alterations was to make layer 1 slightly more similar to layers 2-3, or, in other words, slightly more domesdaylike; and

that is the direction in which we would expect the text to evolve, to the extent that it evolved at all. Of course we do not know whether layer 1 was being altered before the 1120s; but if it was, the alterations are likely to have had the same net effect. Extrapolating backwards, we may suspect that layer 1 would have been even less domesday-like, in its original form, than it is in the earliest form which is known to us.

I do not suggest that this quantitative argument ought to be trusted far, still less that it enables us to calculate a date for layer 1. We cannot expect to form any clear idea of the rate at which the landscape was changing, nor of the rate at which the text was being modified, so as to make it more conformable with reality. Despite all the qualifications which have to be borne in mind, it still seems a fair conclusion to me that the landscape reflected in layer 1 is very much older than Domesday – perhaps a hundred years older, perhaps more.

If we accept that, one other piece of evidence – which, up to this point, would hardly have seemed worth mentioning – now becomes possibly relevant. In two charters surviving from the Christ Church archive, we encounter among the witnesses a man named Gislheard.[37] Both documents are highly problematic; but both witness lists appear to have been derived from charters of king Æthelwulf (839-855). Though we cannot be certain that this Gislheard was the same man who gave his name to the place which the bridgework text calls *Gisleardesland*, the name is uncommon enough for the identification to have some plausibility. If it is valid, the bridgework text cannot be earlier than the mid ninth century. (In fact, I doubt whether anyone would want to think that it might be earlier than that.)

For these reasons, I suggest that layer 1 should be dated to somewhere between 850 and 1000, possibly with some preference for the earlier part of this interval. Within that bracket there is one conjuncture which might be thought to provide a context for the writing of the bridgework text. I hesitate to make the suggestion, because it may be entirely gratuitous. But the reader should, I think, be put in possession of the facts, and invited to consider the possibility.

In 885 an army of Vikings landed in Kent and began an attack on Rochester. Their arrival seems to have come as a surprise, but the city was well enough fortified and manned to defend itself. This was no hit-and-run raid: the Vikings laid siege to the city, and built themselves a fortress. But the city held out; and some time later, with the English army approaching, the Vikings gave up, abandoned their fortress, took to their ships, and sailed away again. Our only account of these events is a few lines of narrative in the *Anglo-Saxon Chronicle*, which leave a great deal unsaid. (We are not told, for instance, why the Vikings thought that Rochester was worth attacking, or why they were prepared to invest their time and energy in a prolonged siege.) Nothing is said about the bridge. From the Vikings' point of view, however, it would look like a sensible plan to disable the bridge straight away, by setting fire to one of the spans, or by tearing up some of the planks.

If that is what happened, the bridge would have needed some reconstruction, once the city had been relieved. The damage done by the Vikings is unlikely to have been any greater than what would occur now and then through natural causes; but on this occasion the circumstances were extraordinary. Extraordinary too was the presence of the king himself, in command of the English army. It seems possible, therefore, that the bridgework text relates to the system of arrangements worked out at this time, after the relief of Rochester, for repairing the bridge immediately, and for keeping it repaired in the future. To the extent that we can make it out, through a palimpsest of later revisions, we may be looking at a document drawn up in the time of – and possibly by order of – king Ælfred.

Spans 6-8

Even in the earliest form which we can visualize, the text is marked by a puzzling dichotomy. Some of the spans are to be repaired by collections of entities of the kind which later came to be called manors, while the other spans are the responsibility of single entities of the kind which later came to be called hundreds. The revisions described above affected the lists of names of manorlike entities; they did not alter this fundamental distinction.

In some places, it seems, there were local arrangements in existence which could be made responsible for repairing parts of the bridge at Rochester. Though not called by this name, they seem to have been similar to hundreds; more than that, they seem to have corresponded (at least partially) with actual hundreds which existed in the late eleventh century.[38] Span 6, we are told, is *to Holinganburnan and to*

eallan þam læþe, 'for Hollingbourne and all the district', which was later construed to mean the hundred of Eyhorne. Spans 7 and 8 are *to Howaran lande to wyrcenne*, 'for the Hoo people's land to construct', which was later taken to signify the hundred of Hoo. Even in the eighteenth century, the distinction implied in the bridgework text still made a practical difference. For the other spans, the burden fell on the tenants of the specified manors, but for these three spans it fell on every house-holder dwelling within the hundred.[39]

Over most of the catchment, by contrast, it appears that no hundredlike arrangements were in existence (or perhaps they existed but had proved to be unreliable).[40] To coordinate the bridgework due from other places, help was available from the three dignitaries who were – *ex officio* – permanent features of the landscape, the king (span 4), the archbishop (spans 5 and 9, perhaps also span 2), and the bishop (spans 1 and 3). Experience had shown, it seems, that some degree of coercion might be necessary; but I do not have any clear understanding of how the arrangement would work.

The question we have to ask – without much hope of being able to answer it – is whether this dichotomy has a chronological significance. Was there once a time when every part of the bridge was assigned to a hundredlike entity? Is there a layer 0, half hidden behind layer 1? In different language from mine, Brooks suggests that there was (though I do not think he means to imply that layer 0 existed in written form); and I agree with him that the suggestion is appealing. The dichotomy is so odd that for that very eason it seems more likely to have evolved – through some of the spans being reallocated to consortia of manorlike entities – rather than to have existed from the beginning.

I see only one indication which might be thought to confirm that something of this sort did happen. The first few words of paragraph 1 do seem to imply that what is about to be explained is an innovation. The bishop of the town, we are told, *fehð ... to wercene*, 'takes to make', the first span. These are everyday words. *Wyrcan* can refer to the making of anything, even something small and delicate, but in this context can best be translated as 'to build' or 'to construct'. *Fehð* is from *fon*, 'to take': by extension it can mean 'to accept some duty', and Robertson's translation, 'undertakes', seems to capture the intended meaning.[41] Thus we are being told that the bishop of the town 'undertakes to construct' the first span.

If somebody is said to 'take' something, we ought to be entitled to infer that it did not belong to him beforehand; so the bishop seems to have been accepting a responsibility which had previously not been his.

Summary

To recapitulate, I suggest that the bridgework text evolved over a long period of time. The earliest form that we can recognize is unlikely to be later than the tenth century, and could be older still. Whatever its date, the text was a formal document, drawn up with the assent of all the parties concerned (including the king), intended to have the force of law; and what it describes is a new arrangement, negotiated between the parties, superseding some earlier arrangement (perhaps similar, perhaps very different) which had proved to be inadequate. The document was entrusted for safekeeping to the church of Rochester – not because it had any religious significance, but because a church was the only place where one could deposit a document with any degree of confidence that the document would still be there in a hundred years' time.

Throughout its existence, the text was open to adjustment, now and then, here and there; but on two occasions at least it underwent some drastic modification. On the first such occasion, around the middle of the eleventh century, the paragraphs concerning spans 5 and 9 (the archbishop's spans) were revised; and perhaps the whole document was written out anew. In this form, in the 1120s, the text was copied into Rochester's cartulary, together with a Latin paraphrase, probably composed somewhat earlier. On the second occasion, around 1200, the paragraphs concerning spans 1 and 3 (the bishop's spans) were revised. That produced the final form of the text – the form which continued to be consulted, as long as the bridge itself remained in existence.

NOTES

1 The publication in question (Thorpe 1731) is a 4-page pamphlet, without author's or printer's name. Copies exist among Thorpe's papers in the library of the Society of Antiquaries and among the records of the Rochester Bridge Trust. Hasted (1782, p. 16) was clearly making use of this pamphlet, though he does not cite it specifically.

2 The seven-mile rule was one of the changes authorized by act of parliament in 1585 (Gibson 1994, pp. 130-2).

3 Loosely speaking, the bridge at Deptford (TQ 3776) might have been said – and was said – to belong to the hundred of Blackheath; but that was not strictly accurate. In the 1340s, an inquiry reported that the whole hundred was liable for the cost of its repair; but somebody must have protested, because a second inquiry was held one year later, and this time it was agreed that in fact the men of Eltham, Mottingham, and Woolwich had never been expected to contribute (*Calendar of inquisitions miscellaneous (Chancery)*, vol. 2, nos. 1929, 1971). Similarly the sixth span of Rochester bridge was loosely said to belong to the hundred of Eyhorne, without that being strictly true (above, p. 8, note 22).

4 In the thirteenth century the men of the hundred of Eyhorne tried to argue that because of their prior commitment to Rochester Bridge they could not be held responsible for mending half of the bridge at Hawkenbury (TQ 7944). On one occasion, it seems, they gained their point; but in 1293, when the matter came up again, the king's justices decided against them (Flower 1915, pp. 198-201, from the Coram Rege roll for Easter 1321, when once again the matter was in dispute). It was generally thought, I infer, that no place ought to have to help with the maintenance of more than one bridge; but government did not accept this as axiomatic.

5 But perhaps it might be possible, from other evidence, to make some progress in piecing the map together. For example, the six places which did have to pay for repairing the bridge at Deptford in the 1340s (above, note 3) were West Greenwich (= Deptford), East Greenwich (= Greenwich), Lewisham, Kidbrooke, Lee, Charlton.

6 This statement includes *Pinindene*, which I would propose to identify, not with Pinden (TQ 5969) in the parish of Horton, but with a lost place of the same name, somewhere in Strood, given to the monks of Rochester in the 1140s (Strood, Rochester upon Medway Studies Centre, DRc/T191/1-3).

7 Brooks (1994, p. 35) seems to be saying that the whole burden of repairing the bishop's spans 'was met from the priory's estates', but that is inaccurate. The manors which belonged to the monks were Frindsbury and Stoke in paragraph 1, Southfleet in paragraph 3; portions of all three were reserved as holdings for the bishop's knights. West Malling, also in paragraph 3, was held by the nuns of Malling, from around 1100 onwards; but the bishops of Rochester retained some degree of control – or so it seems.

8 A particular question arises in the case of Stoke (one of the monks' manors), which, because it belonged to the hundred of Hoo, ought already to have liable for spans 7 and 8. The monks' tenants would hardly have been content to accept a share of the responsibility for span 1 unless in return they were released from this other commitment. If they were excused, however, the other men of Stoke and the other men of the hundred of Hoo would all have had to pay more; and presumably they would have protested. We do not know how this dilemma was resolved.

9 British Library, Cotton Vespasian A.xxii, fols. 65r-70v; Strood, DRc/R2, Custumale Roffense, fols. 9r-15r, probably copied from Vespasian; Thorpe 1788, pp. 1-5, from Custumale. By the 1220s, the Rochester monks had stopped counting in sulungs: the assessments are quoted as numbers of yokes. In the following list, the bracketed pairs of figures are the assessments in yokes reported for the 1080s and 1220s

respectively: Frindsbury (28, 21), Stoke (12, 9), Southfleet (20, 25), Wouldham (12, 10), Denton (2, 3·075). (The second figure for Denton is 3 yokes plus 3 acres; it is clear from the arithmetic that here there were 40 acres in a yoke.) Thus two assessments appear to have been increased, and three to have been reduced; not one remains the same.

10 For example, compare the endorsements on Campbell 1973, no. 17: a tenth-century scribe identified this document as 'Borstal's book', *Borhstealles boc*, a thirteenth-century scribe wrote *Borstalle*. The spelling *Falchenham* would also have seemed old-fashioned from the point of view of a thirteenth-century scribe, but the use of *ch* (to denote a 'k' sound, as in *Chent*) is a distinctively post-conquest feature; the tenth-century spelling would be *Fealcnaham*.

11 What is marked as the parish of Borstal on Brooks's map (1994, fig. 5) is in fact the parish of St Margaret. Borstal did not become a separate parish until the nineteenth century.

12 Domesday Book, fols. 7rb, 8va. All three had existed as separate holdings 'in the time of king Eadward'.

13 Domesday Book, fol. 8va. This is the holding which later came to be known as Malmaynes (TQ 8175). Because it was part of the hundred of Hoo, its tenants would have had to contribute towards spans 7 and 8. Osterland (TQ 8375) also lay within the parish of Stoke, but because it was attached to the manor of Cliffe (owned by the monks of Christ Church) it was taken to belong to the hundred of Shamwell, not the hundred of Hoo (Hasted 1797-1801, vol. 4, p. 34); its tenants would presumably have had to contribute to span 9.

14 The fact that the manor of West Peckham overlapped with the parish of Hadlow gave rise to a fracas in the 1350s, which in turn gave rise to a lawsuit (Flower 1915, p. 208, note 1). The plaintiffs – accused of having caused the trouble themselves by refusing to pay their share – denied 'that any tenant of lands or tenements in Hadlow was liable to contribute'; but that was not the issue in dispute. According to the defendants, these men were not being asked to pay because they held tenements in Hadlow; on the contrary, they were bound to contribute, despite the fact that their tenements were in Hadlow, by virtue of the fact that the tenements were 'held of the manor of West Peckham'. See also note 18.

15 For making sense of layer 3, the map we want, but cannot hope to draw, is a map of the manors existing around 1200. Schematized maps of the parish boundaries existing in the nineteenth century (Ward 1934, p. 15; Brooks 1994, fig. 5) have some value as proxies for this unattainable map, thanks to the inertia in the system; but they are not to be trusted in detail.

16 Here I am assuming that in paragraphs 1 and 3 the changes made respected the preexisting format. Of course we cannot be sure that this is true.

17 On this point Brooks (1994, pp. 18-20) has said all that needs to be said. The case is closed; and I for one have no intention of opening it up again.

18 The name Hazelholt does occur in Domesday Book, but only as somebody's surname: in one of the prefatory paragraphs we hear of a woman (alive in the time of king Eadward) called 'Eadgith of Hazelholt', *Edid de Aisiholte* (fol. 1va). According to Thorpe (1731, p. 2), Hazelholt was 'supposed to be the manor

of Hilthe in or near Nettlested'; but I do not know of any evidence in favour of this supposition. The identification of *Hæselholt* with Hadlow, taken for granted by Brooks, was first proposed by Ward (1932). His reasons were mistaken or unconvincing, as Wallenberg (1934, p. 176) pointed out; and I cannot see why Ward's guess should continue to be allowed the benefit of the doubt. As regards the question of bridgework, we happen to know that the men of Hadlow were – by and large – not required to contribute towards the repair of Rochester bridge (above, note 14). If we want more proof, we need look no further than the report of the 1340 inquiry (Appendix 2, no. 4). This gives a list of the places responsible for repairing the fifth span. Hadlow is not on the list. Hazelholt and Swanton are both omitted, with the implication that they had ceased to exist as separate places. Their share of the burden may have been transferred to other places (below, note 21), but plainly it had not been transferred to Hadlow.

19 For Wateringbury, Domesday Book reports two holdings of 2 sulungs each (fol. 8vb); for Offham, two holdings of 1 sulung each (fol. 7rb-va).

20 In both cases, Brooks's (1992, pp. 19-20) arithmetic is faulty. The figures he gives add up to 50 (not 49) sulungs for 'pier' 5 and 43·875 (not 43·75) sulungs for 'pier' 9. The first total includes 6 sulungs for Hadlow, which I do not count, because I reject the identification with *Hæselholt* (above, note 18); the second total includes a privately owned half-sulung holding at Cliffe, which again I do not count, because we are told explicitly that the holding liable for bridgework is the one belonging to the archbishop ('his Cliffe').

21 The report of an inquiry held on 1 March 1340 (Appendix 2, no. 4) provides us with an updated list of the places responsible for repairing the fifth span, together with the number of sulungs for which each place was answerable. *Hæselholt* and *Swanatun* are omitted (above, note 18), and several of the assessments have been adjusted, mostly in a downward direction. The total comes to 34·5 sulungs. In fact, there is only one assessment which has been increased: Wateringbury, which appears in Domesday Book as two holdings of 2 sulungs each (above, note 19), is assessed at 7 sulungs here. It is conceivable that *Hæselholt* and *Swanatun* had been swallowed up (before the 1080s) by the manor of Wateringbury, and that Wateringbury's assessment was eventually increased (after the 1080s) to take account of this fact. But I do not press the suggestion.

22 This is the opinion of Mr P. R. Kitson, cited by Brooks (1994, pp. 363-4). One point not mentioned by Kitson, but possibly of some significance, is the substitution of *u* for *f* (to denote a 'v' sound), instances of which occur in the portion of the text written by the main scribe (*syoueþe, cliue*) as well as in the rewritten portion (*hrouecæstre, trotescliue*). This is common in the late eleventh century, and normal in the twelfth; but I do not know that it starts happening before about the 1040s (e.g. Robertson 1939, no. 103 = Sawyer 1968, no. 1473).

23 There are many intermediate forms, and they cannot be arranged into any single sequence. One possible trajectory would be *Hrofesceastre* > *Hrofeceastre* > *Rofeceastre* > *Rofecestre* > *Rouecestre*.

24 For example, Robertson 1939, no. 75 (= Sawyer 1968, no. 1220). The substitution of *æ* for *e* before *n* is a common Kentish trait (Campbell 1973, p. xxx), and occurs once elsewhere in the bridgework text (*ænde* for *ende*).

25 If they were part of the list, then in 'classical' spelling they ought to read *and to eallum þam dennwarum*.

26 Another document from the Rochester archive (Flight 1996, p. 141) seems to prove – by implication – that Aylesford belonged to the king in the 990s. The same evidence is relevant for Chalk.

27 Obviously, this cannot be the same lathe of Aylesford which formed part of the topographical framework for the Domesday survey: the lathe referred to here has to be something much smaller. There was apparently still some recognized meaning attached to this phrase at the end of the twelfth century. In 1197, when the sheriff of Kent was squaring his account with the Exchequer, he claimed two deductions with respect to Aylesford: £26 'in Aylesford', because the holding which would normally have paid this rent to him had been given to the count of Mortain (the king's brother Johan), plus £6 'in the lathe of the same place (*in lesto eiusdem uille*)' which had been given to Willelm de Caiho (*Pipe roll 9 Richard I*, p. 25). The usual rent paid to the sheriff from Aylesford was £32 in total. So this 'lathe' appears to have been a distinct entity, dependent on Aylesford but detachable from it; and the bridgework text, by referring to the 'lathe' explicitly, seems to have had the intention of making it clear that the name 'Aylesford' should be construed in the largest sense, not in the narrower sense which would exclude the 'lathe'.

28 I include the four names erased from *Privilegia* but preserved in the Hollingbourne memorandum (above, p. 3).

29 In Domesday Book (fol. 7rb) Eccles is assessed at 3 yokes; by around 1230 its assessment had dwindled to 25 acres (Brooks 1994, p. 368). (The name *Ecclesse* does still appear in the 1343 report (Appendix 2, no. 5), but it has been misread as 'church' in the printed synopsis.) By the eighteenth century the manor had disintegrated, and the site of the manor-house had been forgotten (Hasted 1797-1801, vol. 4, p. 434). The Eccles which appears on modern maps (TQ 7260) is, I believe, a company village, created on a vacant site in the nineteenth century. I do not know how it got its name, nor whether it occupies the same site as the medieval manor.

30 Assessed at only one sulung in the Hollingbourne memorandum (Appendix 2, no. 1), so perhaps meaning just West Farleigh, where one sulung was divided into two privately owned holdings (Domesday Book, fol. 8va-b). East Farleigh, which belonged to the monks of Canterbury, was assessed at 6 sulungs (fol. 4vb); it had swallowed up two places – Loose and Linton – which are listed separately here (below, note 34).

31 Called *Ædun* in the rewritten part of the English version, *Hathdune* in the Latin version, *Hadone* in Domesday Book (fol. 9ra); assessed at ¼ sulung in the Hollingbourne memorandum (where the name appears in the mangled form *Hondene*); omitted from the 1343 report. Identified by Thorpe (1731, pp. 2, 3), with the manor of Haydon (TQ 6769) in Cobham; but that seems very doubtful. A ninth-century charter survives (Sawyer 1968, no. 1276) relating to land at *Haddun*, presumably the same place, with the right of access to meadows at Beckley (TQ 7074) and Strood (TQ 7369), i.e. in the floodplains on either side of the isthmus between the Thames and the Medway. Wallenberg (1931, pp. 227-32) proposed to identify *Haddun* with Haven Street (TQ 7471) in Frindsbury, but that does not appear to be anything more than a guess.

32 Not 'Cozenton' (Brooks 1992, p. 18; 1994, p. 33, note 78): that spelling belongs to the place (TQ 8166) near Rainham, not the place (TQ 7459) near Aylesford.

33 The identification of *Dudesland* with Dode (TQ 6663) was first proposed by Ward (1932, 1934). It involves two lemmas: that *Dudes land* was the place of which *Dodes circe* (*Privilegia*, fol. 221r) was the church; and that *Dodes circe* was the same church that was later called just *Dode*. The second point seems fairly secure, but the first is just a guess.

34 From 'Domesday Monachorum', fol. 4vc (ed. Douglas 1944, p. 95), and from *Privilegia*, fol. 220v, it seems that Loose and Linton had both become absorbed into the manor of East Farleigh. Separate assessments of 1 sulung and 2 sulungs respectively are reported in the Hollingbourne memorandum.

35 This is one of the names erased from *Privilegia*. In the Hollingbourne memorandum it appears as *Lichebundelonde* (Brooks 1994, p. 368). By analogy with the spellings *Glislardelande* and *Gliselardelonde* for 'Gislheard's land', I take *Lichebund* to be a blundered form of an antiquated personal name.

36 If Gillingham and Chatham are included in layer 2 (above, p. 16), the first entry in the second column will increase to 23, and the totals will have to be adjusted accordingly.

37 As was noted by Robertson (1939, p. 353); these are the only two instances of the name recorded in Birch's index. The charters in question are Birch 1885-93, nos. 536, 538 (= Sawyer 1968, nos. 344, 319). The former is the work of Brooks's scribe 7 (Brooks 1984, p. 172).

38 Ward (1934) thought that the hundred of Chatham might also be represented (span 2). The places named are Gillingham and Chatham, which certainly did belong to the hundred of Chatham. But in Thorpe's understanding of the case the burden here fell, not on the parishes, but on the manors – which were far from being coextensive with the parishes whose names they shared. In fact, one of the other manors lying within the parish of Chatham is named elsewhere in the text: Horsted is listed among the places liable for span 4. It seems a likelier theory to me that span 2 was, initially, one of the spans put under the archbishop's supervision (above, p. 16).

39 In the eighteenth century the hundred of Hoo comprised the parishes of Hoo, Halstow, St Mary Hoo, Allhallows, and Stoke, minus a small part of Stoke, plus small parts of Cobham and West Peckham (Hasted 1797-1801, vol. 4, p. 2). By that time, Allhallows and West Peckham had escaped liability for Rochester bridge, thanks to the seven-mile rule (above, note 2); but where the burden still existed, it fell on 'the whole parish, as lying within the hundred of Hoo' (Thorpe 1731, pp. 3-4). The same applied to Eyhorne. Nearly all the hundred had escaped liability by then, through the same loophole; but one parish had been trapped, namely Bredhurst, and here too the burden fell on 'the whole parish, as lying within the hundred of Eyhorne'.

40 There seems to be no correlation between the groups of places named in layers 2-3 and the administrative districts existing in the eleventh century. The catchments for the archbishop's two spans are spatially disjunct (Fig. 4), but the dividing line between them bisects the hundred of Larkfield; and other places in the same hundred were liable for work on (the king's) span 4 or (the bishop's) span 3, while others again were

not liable at all. In a very similar way, the catchments for the bishop's two spans are spatially disjunct (Fig. 3), but the dividing line between them bisects the hundred of Shamwell; and other places in the same hundred were liable for work on (the king's) span 4 or (the archbishop's) span 9, while others again were not liable at all. Perhaps someone else can see sense in this, but I have stopped trying.

41 The word *fon* can also mean 'to begin (to do something)': the Latin version says *incipit operari*, 'begins to work', perhaps with the idea that the bishop 'starts things off' by building the first span.

3

Interpretations

Even in its original form, the bridgework text was not the sort of text which can properly be said to have had an author. No single person was responsible for its wording. Nevertheless, there did exist, somewhere in the past, an individual intelligence behind each word. If we want to understand the original meaning of the text, we have to try to communicate with this intelligence.

It seems clear, first, that the arrangements described here were not intended to provide for the minor repairs and routine maintenance which any bridge — especially a wooden bridge — is bound to need. What do we think was supposed to happen, for instance, in (say) the mid eleventh century, if a plank came loose in span 6? It cannot be thought that a messenger was sent to Hollingbourne, that the men of Hollingbourne discussed the matter at their next monthly meeting, and that somebody was chosen who (weather permitting) would travel to Rochester, nail down the plank, and then go home again. There must have been some arrangement in place which could cope with such minor repairs. Again, what do we think would happen in winter when the deck became covered with snow? It cannot be thought that everybody sat and watched, waiting for the snow to melt. There must have been somebody whose job it was to make sure that the snow was cleared. That person, I suppose, was the reeve in charge of the town, the *portgerefa*.[1] Most of the time, it would have been the reeve's responsibility to make sure that the bridge was kept functioning.

Second, the arrangements described in the bridgework text were meant to be activated only when the bridge was damaged to the extent of being put out of action — in a word, when it was broken. The Latin version says this explicitly: 'This document shows plainly from which places the bridge of Rochester should be repaired as often as it gets broken (*quotiens fuerit fractus*)'. That was the interpretation placed on the text in the twelfth century; and I think we may assume that it was also the original intention, simply because the arrangements are so cumbersome that they must have been designed for extraordinary purposes. Whether the bridge was broken or not

would often be a matter of fact: if an entire span collapsed, for example, there would not be any room for doubt. But it is easy to imagine that the bridge might sometimes be damaged to a lesser extent, enough perhaps to be impassable to wheeled vehicles, but not to pedestrians, if they were brave or reckless enough to make their way across. At a time like this, somebody — the reeve, I suppose — would have to decide whether the bridge was officially broken or not. The bridgework text is telling us what ought to happen in these abnormal (though probably not uncommon) circumstances.

Third, the text was not concerned with the provision of beams and planking. It was concerned with the provision of labour. The wording is plain enough, and up to a point its meaning is well understood. The word *geweorc* means 'labour-service' (in Brooks's translation); the clause *þe man hi of scæl weorcan* means 'which must supply the labour' (Robertson), 'from which the labour is due' (Brooks). The beams are *to leccanne*, i.e. to be laid, 'put in position' (Robertson), 'set in place' (Brooks); and the sections of the deck are *to pilianne*, i.e. to be covered with planking. The word *pilian* occurs only rarely, and its meaning is therefore not very well attested; but the author of the Latin version translated it as *plancas ponere*, 'to lay planks', and there is no reason to think that he was wrong. In the Hollingbourne memorandum the corresponding word is *plancare*, 'to plank'; and 'to plank' is how Brooks translates the word *pilian* in the bridgework text. In short, the text is telling us who ought to do the work. It does not tell us — it does not try to tell us — who should provide the timber.[2]

Yet that distinction has frequently been lost sight of. In translating the text, Brooks seems to me to capture the meaning correctly; in discussing it, however, he repeatedly speaks as if it dealt with the provision of matériel. Robertson's translation is right about the beams ('to put in position') but wrong about the planking ('to provide planks'). The same confusion occurs in Essex's paper (1785, p. 398), and even further back. According to the report which underlies the Hollingbourne memorandum, when the first span needed repair the bishop of Rochester 'ought to find three beams (*debet inuenire tres sulliues*)' (Brooks 1994, p. 367); and 'find' would seem to imply that the bishop was responsible for procuring the beams and transporting them to the site. But the Exchequer, by that time, was determined to make sure that the whole cost of all repairs was carried by the local population, and the weasel word 'find' has to be read in that light. In some of the derivative texts, all mention of the planking and the beams has been omitted; and even where these specifications are retained, they are never amplified or clarified in any way. These, clearly, were not the details which mattered. For the king's agents there was only one relevant question: which places could be made to pay a share of the cost?

Despite its being misunderstood (more or less purposely) by medieval bureaucrats and (not purposely) by modern scholars, the original intention of the text is not is any doubt. It tells us something about the mobilization of labour, nothing about the procurement of matériel. The question then arises: if it was not really up to the bishop to 'find' any of the beams for the first span, whose responsibility was it? That is a good question, but the bridgework text is not about to tell us the answer. We can only guess; and my guess would be that this was the king's responsibility. It has to be remembered, moreover, that timber would not be the only matériel required. The workmen would have to be provided with boats, ladders, ropes, tools, nails, and possibly all sorts of other things. Again, they would have to be housed and fed, for the duration of the work. It was, I assume, the reeve of Rochester, as the king's representative on the spot, who dealt with all these organizational matters, including the procurement of timber.

Beyond all that, there is the necessity for expertise. The *portgerefa* may have had many talents, but he would not have been a craftsman. The labour recruited from the surrounding country would not have been experienced in building bridges. To plan and supervise the work, a skilled carpenter would be required — one at least, preferably two or three. Again, I would guess that it was the king's business to make sure that a competent craftsman took charge of the work.

If part of the seventh span collapsed, what do we think would happen? Something like this, I suppose. The reeve of the town inspected the damage, declared the bridge to be broken, and notified higher

authority. His first priority was to organize a ferry service, to last for as long as the bridge was out of action. As soon as possible, he obtained the services of a qualified carpenter, who could advise him exactly what was needed in the way of timber, equipment, and so on; and he set in train the arrangements (whatever they were) for obtaining these supplies. Meanwhile, he sent a message to the people of Hoo, ordering them to mobilize a certain number of men, and reminding them of the penalties they would face if any of the men should fail to present themselves in Rochester on the appointed day. At their next meeting, the people of Hoo decided which men should be sent; and in due course these men made their way to Rochester, reporting to the reeve when they arrived.

This is all guesswork, and I am perfectly willing to believe that all of it is wrong. The point is that we find ourselves reduced to guessing precisely because the bridgework text does not provide us with any information. The purpose of the text was to tell us something about the mobilization of unskilled labour; and that is what it does. But this procedure does not make sense except as one component in a larger system of arrangements, concerning the rest of which we know practically nothing.

Readings and misreadings

Even where the bridgework text appears to be telling us something explicitly and unambiguously, there is still a risk of our misunderstanding it. In a word, we are at cross purposes with the author (if we may briefly think of him as such). The readers he had in ind were people — unlike us — who knew what the bridge was like, or, if they did not know, could find out for themselves by the simple expedient of going to take a look at it. Thus the author assumes that the bridge itself will illustrate his text. By and large, he does not tell his readers the obvious things, because those he expects them to know; he tells them the things which — in his view — they cannot be expected to know without being told.

In particular, when the author speaks of three beams for each span, we cannot construe him to mean that three was the total number.[3] On the contrary, if that had been what he meant to say, the author would not have needed to mention the number at all: he could simply have said 'to lay the beams' — or, if he wished to be more emphatic, 'to lay all the beams' — and felt sure of being understood correctly. By specifying a number, the author is telling us this:

that out of the total number of beams (which we are assumed to be capable of counting for ourselves) three are to be laid by the labourers from Hoo (or from Hollingbourne, or from whatever lands are named in connection with this span). Thus we are caught in a paradox: the fact that the author mentions a number is proof that this was not the total number. We cannot expect the text to tell us what the total number was, except, of course, that it must have been greater than three.

In any case, for the engineering reasons discussed in more detail elsewhere (below, Appendix 3), it is unthinkable that the deck was supported by three beams alone. For a footbridge across a stream, three wooden beams would be adequate; for an important roadbridge across a large river, three is a ridiculous number. In Essex's reconstruction (below, p. 43), each span is carried by eight beams. His reasons for deciding on eight beams exactly were, without question, wrong; but they were not arbitrary. Unlike most of the rest of us, Essex had practical experience of designing and constructing bridges. He was a builder and a carpenter, as well as an architect: he knew how to put together a timber deck, with some confidence that it would serve its purpose and last for a respectable length of time. If Essex tells us that eight beams would be about the right number, I for one am not competent to disagree with him. It thus appears that the labour supplied in accordance with the bridgework text was only a fraction – probably less than half – of the total labour required. That is a puzzling conclusion; but I think it must be right.

The same sort of argument which applies to the beams will also apply to the planks. If the quantities of planking had coincided in any obvious way with the structural divisions of the bridge, it would not have been necessary for the quantities to be specified. By spelling out these measurements, the author implies that he has some reason for thinking that they need to be spelt out; and unless we can see what that reason was, we are not going to understand what the measurements mean.

It certainly cannot be true that by adding up all the measurements given we arrive at the total length of the bridge, namely 26·5 rods. As far as I know, we do not have any exact indication what was meant by a rod before the thirteenth century, when it becomes clear – from evidence of the kind discussed by Witney (1992) – that a rod in Kent was generally reckoned to be equivalent to 16 feet. There are some

clues suggesting that it varied locally, but none that it varied by more than a small amount. By that reckoning, we are going to decide that the bridge was 424 feet long. But that is not credible. A bridge of that length would not extend from one side of the river to the other; and a bridge which fails to do that is not a bridge at all.

Nor can these figures be taken to imply that that the spans varied in length by a factor of four – i.e. to the extent that the longest span was four times as long as the shortest.[4] That is a ridiculous idea. For reasons explained elsewhere (below, Appendix 3), the performance of a wooden deck depends very sensitively on the length of the span. An engineer designing such a bridge is more or less compelled to adopt a modular plan, with the supports placed at equal distances. Simply because the bridge had a wooden deck, we can take it for granted – as Essex did – that the spans were all equal in length, or very nearly so.[5]

Yet there is some sign that the amount of labour (or cash in lieu) likely to be required was expected to vary, from one span to the next, more or less in proportion to the numbers of rods of planking. The smallest quantity of planking is a single rod for span 2, which 'belongs to Gillingham and Chatham'; and the assessments reported for these two manors are 6 sulungs each,[6] giving a total of 12. By contrast, for spans 5 and 9, perhaps in the same layer of text (above, p. 16) and each said to have four rods of planking, the number of sulungs responsible adds up to more than 40 in either case (Table 1). Thus Brooks (1994, p. 31) does seem to be right – at least for these three spans – in thinking that the number of sulungs was intended to be roughly proportional to the number of rods of planking (which varies from span to span), rather than to the number of beams (which is constant).

The suggestion that I am about to make does not sound very convincing, even to me, but I cannot think of a better one. The measurements of planking may perhaps be fossilized remnants, surviving from an earlier arrangement which related only to the deck itself, not to the supporting structures (i.e. the stone piers and timber frames). Through some sequence of historical accidents, I suggest, the roadway had come to be divided into eight unequal segments.[7] For example, one segment – the longest of all – was assigned to the men of Hoo: if some portion of the planking here needed to be replaced, they supplied the labour. Then the arrangement was modified so that it also made provision for repairs to the timber frames.[8] The groups of people responsible for the segments of planking were each made responsible for contributing to one of the spans as well – except the men of Hoo, who had to contribute to two. This revised arrangement is the one embodied in the bridgework text.

That the text should be so difficult to understand is disappointing perhaps, but really not surprising. Like any author, the author of this text assumed that his readers would possess (or be able to acquire) a certain level of background knowledge. He cannot be blamed for failing to realize that some of his readers would be ignoramuses like us. By the same token, we ought not to blame ourselves too harshly if we have to admit that in some respects the text is incomprehensible.

The official reading

By the fourteenth century, whatever may have been true in the distant past, nobody had any ex-officio responsibility for making sure that the bridge was in good repair; nor was there any revenue available for the purpose.[9] In theory, the city was leased to the citizens. They were allowed to make themselves responsible for collecting the rents, tolls and other profits which belonged to the king, paying a fixed amount into the Exchequer each year, and keeping the balance (if there was one) for themselves. In their dealings with the king they were represented by two elected bailiffs. The city's first charter, stipulating a rent of £25, dates from 1227 (*Calendar of charter rolls 1226-57*, p. 64); but in fact we can tell, from entries on the pipe rolls, that the citizens started paying this rent at the Exchequer in the financial year ending at Michaelmas 1192 (*Pipe rolls 3-4 Richard I*, pp. 307-8).[10]

From time to time, the arrangement was interrupted. If ever a king felt justified in doing so, he could 'take the city into his hands' at a moment's notice. That happened, for instance, in 1261, because of 'the troubles in the realm' (below, p. 39); and it happened again in 1272 (*Calendar of patent rolls 1266-72*, p. 642). Furthermore, from 1280 onwards, despite what the charters say, the 'farm of the city' was granted for life, jointly with the 'keeping of the castle', to a succession of individual entrepreneurs, beginning with John de Cobham.[11] Under this arrangement the bailiff of the city was not elected by the citizens: he was appointed, and paid a salary, by the keeper of the city.[12] The citizens did not

regain control till 1438 (*Calendar of charter rolls 1427-1516*, pp. 2-4).

It is clear that none of the money collected at Rochester on the king's behalf was required to be spent on the upkeep of the bridge. When repairs were needed, it was never the citizens who were expected to make them; nor was it the keeper of the city. As for the money which was forwarded to the Exchequer, there was little chance of that being seen in Rochester again. Most of the time, it had been promised to somebody, even before it was received.[13] On occasions when the bridge was out of action, people had to use the officially licensed ferry, and they had to pay for doing so.[14] In principle, the contract for operating the ferry could be awarded to anyone, and the profits could be disposed of in any way. Each time, the king decided.[15] There were no precedents which he was bound to respect, nor any presumption that he would let the profits from the ferry be spent on repairing the bridge.[16]

By the fourteenth century, the archbishop and bishop were no longer being expected to involve themselves with the maintenance of the bridge; central government had taken full charge. From the changes made, around 1200, in the arrangements relating to spans 1 and 3 (above, p. 12), it seems clear that the bishop of Rochester was, at that time, still being held responsible for the spans allotted to him by the bridgework text; and presumably the same applied to the archbishop too. Around 1230, we find the relevant information incorporated into the report which forms the basis for the Hollingbourne memorandum, as if it still had some practical significance. After that, the archbishop and bishop disappear from the record. In 1310-11, when some of the men of Westerham failed to pay their share of the cost of repairing the bridge, it was the king's bailiff who attempted to distrain their property, and, when a fracas ensued, it was the sheriff who was ordered to investigate the incident (*Calendar of inquisitions miscellaneous (Chancery)*, vol. 2, p. 26). The men of Westerham were liable for the repair of span 5, one of the spans which in theory came under the archbishop's superintendence; but clearly that had ceased to be true in practice.

Whenever the bridge needed repair, the king appointed a commission of local notables, with orders to decide what work was required, and to make sure that the work got done. The sheriff was instructed to cooperate with the commissioners, but was not expected to act on his own initiative. Though the same commissioners often served on more than one occasion, this simply means that the pool of qualified candidates was fairly small: nobody incurred any permanent responsibility by participating in one, or even in several, of these inquiries. Once the work had been completed, the commission lapsed; the next time repairs were needed, the machinery had to be set in motion all over again.

Central government did not take the view that the provisions described in the bridgework text were intended to be activated only when the bridge was in need of some major reconstruction – i.e. when it was 'broken'. The official interpretation was that all repairs, large or small, had to be paid for locally. It is difficult to see how the men of dozens of different places could be expected to organize themselves into carrying out routine maintenance on the bridge at Rochester; but that is what their duty was construed to be. Hence, if the bridge was ever out of repair, that fact was instant proof of negligence on their part. Now they were caught twice over. They were not just compelled to pay for the repairs: they were also at risk of being penalized for having failed in their duty.

We can take it for granted that the system for exacting money for the bridge provoked some resentment and some recalcitrance on the part of the people on whom the burden fell. It is not to be thought that everybody always paid up willingly and promptly. For many people the system must have seemed manifestly unjust. On one occasion, the men of Westerham made an effort to get themselves released from their obligation to Rochester bridge (Appendix 2, no. 4). We do not know what arguments they employed, but we do know how much success they had: none at all.[17] As Brooks (1994, p. 30) comments, there was 'no appeal against the evidence of the bridgework list, however unreasonable it might be'. If the men of Westerham, furthest from the bridge, were unable to dent the system, it would surely have been a waste of time for other people to try. Presumably they realized that and kept their mouths shut; but there must have been many places where people had some reason for feeling aggrieved – for wondering why they should be forced to pay, while other people, closer to the bridge, were not.

Only a few figures are recorded, and I not see that we can make much sense of them. In 1343 it was estimated that the repairs which were needed would cost at least £19 for the first span and £8 6s 8d for the third; in the other spans there were 'no defects'

to report (Appendix 2, no. 5). Only twelve years later, in 1355, every single span was said to be in need of repair, and the total cost was estimated at more than £500 (Appendix 2, no. 6).[18] This is, as Brooks says, 'an astonishing sum' (1994, p. 39), all the more astonishing by comparison with the 1343 report, which seems to be telling us that most of the bridge was in fairly good condition at the time, and that the two defective spans were about to be made good. I find it hard to imagine how it would have been possible even to think of spending so much money on the bridge. It has to be remembered, of course, that the figures which we are given are only estimates: we have no means of knowing how much was actually spent.

Nevertheless, it seems fair to say that the financial burden was heavy, and perhaps becoming heavier.[19] In response, some sort of informal arrangement seems to have been worked out for money to be collected and saved, against the time when it would next be demanded. From the 1350s onwards, whenever commissioners were appointed to repair the bridge, there was a clause in the king's letter empowering them to lay their hands on this money.[20] A document submitted to parliament in November 1391 reports that the places responsible for the bridge 'were accustomed to choose two men from among themselves' to supervise its repair and manage its affairs;[21] and these, I suppose, are the men who were thought likely to have unspent funds in their possession. In May 1311, just after the structure had been made good 'at great expense', two local men were appointed by the king 'to be supervisors and keepers of the bridge of Rochester'.[22] This seems to be the only occasion when any formal appointment of the kind was made; but it is possible that wardens began being chosen, unofficially, from this time onwards – or perhaps from 1340 onwards, when once again the bridge broke and had to be repaired.

In some quarters, the system was sure to find support. The Exchequer was in favour of the existing arrangement, as it would have been of any arrangement which meant that repairs were paid for locally, not out of central funds. The citizens of Rochester were doubtless happy to have their bridge maintained at no cost to themselves. And the lords and tenants of all the places which were lucky enough not to be mentioned in the bridgework text had an obvious interest in perpetuating an arrangement which worked to their advantage.[23] Over and over again, inquiries were held, but they always produced the same answer: everybody must have known in advance what the report would say. Still, there were formalities which had to be gone through with, before the sheriff and his agents could be let loose. For government there were only two options: either to overhaul the whole system (as the bishop had tried to do for the spans which belonged to him), or else to enforce it. Coercion was the policy chosen. Whenever commissioners were appointed to supervise repairs to the bridge, they were authorized to use any means necessary to ensure that the people who ought to pay did pay.

For all its defects, the system does seem to have been made to work successfully. After being deliberately disabled in 1264,[24] the bridge was broken in 1282,[25] broken in 1310,[26] broken in 1339 (above, p. 3); but after that preemptive repairs, carried out at frequent intervals, seem to have kept it functioning more or less all the time, for a period of forty years.[27] As far as we know, a ferry was in operation only twice: for three days in 1343 (E 101/507/1), and for three weeks in 1361 (E 101/509/2). On both occasions the shortness of the interruption would seem to imply that the bridge had been, not accidentally broken, but purposely closed to traffic, so that some scheduled repair could be carried out.

Because of the unevenness of the evidence, I do not see how it can be argued that the structure of the bridge was suffering some chronic deterioration during the fourteenth century.[28] A wooden bridge, even if it is well constructed and well looked after, cannot be expected to last for very long. In a manner of speaking, the bridge at Rochester consisted of nine wooden bridges, the failure of any one of which would be enough to disable the entire structure. The frequency with which the bridge was demanding attention during the fourteenth century is not obviously in excess of what one might expect, even if the bridge was in the prime of life.

It is possible that traffic was heavier in the fourteenth century than at any earlier period; and that, if true, would certainly make a difference. In 1311, just after the bridge had been repaired, somebody had the thought that it might be wise 'to prevent wagons too heavily laden from crossing it';[29] but it is not clear that any regulations were drawn up, still less that they were enforced. In any case, we cannot say whether this was a new idea, or an old idea which had not been put into writing until this moment.

NOTES

1 I am not aware of any pre-conquest evidence which proves for a fact that Rochester had a *portgerefa* (as Canterbury did). In the twelfth century, however, the 'king's reeve' (*prepositus regis*) and 'reeveship' (*prepositura*) are mentioned frequently.

2 There is an added sentence at the end of the Latin version stipulating that the beams should be of adequate size for the load they would have to carry – a vague remark, but sensible so far as it goes. Whoever wrote these words was thinking about the provision of matériel; he would seem to have been aware that beams of inadequate size had sometimes been supplied. But the syntax is impersonal (*Et sciendum est*, 'And let it be known'), and we do not know who was issuing this instruction, or who was supposed to be listening, or who was going to decide whether the beams were of acceptable size or not.

3 The text was misunderstood in this way by the contributor who wrote the account of the bridge in Fisher's *History* (below, p. 46, note 4).

4 The text was first misread in this way by Samuel Denne, though only in a private letter, without any thought that his letter might one day be published, as in fact it was (below, p. 37).

5 Besides, even if the spans did vary significantly, it is entirely unlikely that their lengths would all be exact multiples of half a rod.

6 Domesday Book, fols. 3va, 8va. There was also a privately owned half-sulung in Gillingham (fol. 8rb-va), which I take it should not be counted.

7 But this will not seem a credible suggestion unless we are also willing to believe that the measuring-rod being used was roughly 19-20 feet in length. In the 1390s, when arrangements for the maintenance of the new bridge were being discussed (Britnell 1994, pp. 50-1), one proposal was for the bridge to be divided into eight unequal segments, the lengths of which bore no relation whatever to the actual structure (consisting of eleven roughly equal spans) but were calculated – to within an eighth of an inch – so as to be proportional to the numbers of rods of planking quoted in the bridgework text. The new bridge was reckoned to be slightly more than 566 feet long, so each half-rod of planking in the old bridge was made to correspond to a length of 10 feet 8 inches (plus a fraction) in the new bridge. In different circumstances, knowing nothing about the old bridge, we might now be trying to puzzle out what these numbers could possibly mean; and we should be wasting our time.

8 This chronological distinction might perhaps explain why it is that the bridgework text consistently mentions the planking before the beams, when logic would seem to favour the opposite order. But that is a small point, possibly not in need of explanation at all.

9 On just one occasion that we know of, the sheriff was authorized to have the bridge repaired at the cost of the Exchequer. In the pipe roll for 1130 we find the sheriff credited with 3s 4d spent 'on mending the bridge of Rochester in advance of the king's arrival', *in ponte de Rouec' reficiendo contra aduentum regis* (*Pipe roll 31 Henry I*, p. 64). The king was in Rochester on Thursday 8 May 1130, attending the dedication of the cathedral church, and presumably that is the visit referred to here. However, the circumstances were special, the amount was small,

and the Exchequer seems to have ensured that no precedent was created. If the next roll had survived, we might perhaps have learnt what reprisals were taken against the places which had failed to carry out the maintenance required.

10 In the 1180s and before, the 'farm of Rochester' was one of the items of income accounted for by the sheriff under the general heading: 'Farm of the land of the bishop of Bayeux'. Apparently this means that Rochester's *feorm*, in the mid eleventh century, was paid to the *eorl* alone (not shared between the king and the *eorl*, as at Canterbury and Dover), and that it reverted to the crown, with the other perquisites of the *eorldom*, after bishop Odo's arrest in 1082. The 'farm of the land of the bishop of Bayeux' disappears from the pipe rolls after 1189; the 'farm of Rochester' appears for the first time three years later; I do not know what was happening in the interim.

11 *Calendar of patent rolls 1272-81*, p. 376; *Calendar of fine rolls 1272-1307*, p. 128. This is the John de Cobham who died in 1300 (below, note 23). After that the appointment was held briefly by Richard de Gravesende, bishop of London (d. 1303), and then by Cobham's son Henry and grandson John till 1354 (*Calendar of patent rolls 1354-8*, p. 22). Subsequent keepers of the city and castle (with the dates of their appointment) were William de Clinton, earl of Huntingdon (March 1354), Geoffrey de Say (September 1354), John de Grey of Codnor (1359), Simon de Burgh (1370), John de Newenton (1379), William de Arundell (1394), Richard de Arundell (1401). In November 1422 the castle and town were among the properties granted to queen Katherine, the widow of Henry V (*Rotuli parliamentorum*, vol. 4, pp. 184-5; cf. *Calendar of patent rolls 1422-9*, p. 17); it was when she died, in January 1437, that the citizens saw their opportunity.

12 *Calendar of inquisitions miscellaneous (Chancery)*, vol. 2, pp. 307-8, no. 1256, the report of an inquiry into the grievances of the citizens and commonalty of Rochester, held at Dartford on 23 May 1331. The citizens were found to have no cause for complaint; but they dissociated themselves from the verdict.

13 In 1331, for instance, the rent due to the Exchequer 'for the castle and city of Rochester' was one of the items of income assigned to the king's mother (*Calendar of patent rolls 1330-34*, pp. 225-6). She died in 1358. After that the rent was assigned to the king's eldest daughter (*Calendar of patent rolls 1358-61*, p. 200).

14 A day-by-day record of the receipts from the ferry survives for 1339-40 (E 101/507/20); the totals are known for 1343 and 1361 (E 101/507/1, E 101/509/2). The ferry was expected to be big enough to carry carts, as well as people and horses; at least that was true in 1339-40 and 1361.

15 In 1310, for instance, the profits from the ferry were given to one of the king's attendants (*Calendar of patent rolls 1307-13*, pp. 232, 233); by mistake, some of the money was paid into the Exchequer (*Calendar of Chancery warrants*, p. 333), but none of it stayed in Rochester.

16 A share of the proceeds had to be paid to the monks of Rochester − or so the monks asserted. The charters cited by Brooks (1994, p. 35, note 83) are both spurious in my opinion; but a papal privilege of 1155 (Holtzmann 1935-6, pp. 265-8) records that the monks are entitled to 'a quarter share of the crossing of the river when the bridge is broken', *fracto ponte transitus aque quartam partem*. The papal chancery did not

inquire into the validity of such claims: it assumed that it was being told the truth, and safeguarded its own credibility by adding some formulaic qualifications. But the king's justices did investigate the matter thoroughly in 1279, and again in 1313 (Illingworth and Caley 1818, pp. 351, 320-1). On the first occasion the claim was allowed because a jury of local men swore that it was justified; on the second occasion the claim was allowed because it had been allowed before. In 1362, for certain, the 'fourth penny' was paid to the monks: the king's writ, dated 10 October 1362, ordering the payment to be made, and a receipt from the prior and convent, dated 7 November, are both stitched to the account of the proceeds from the ferry (E 101/509/2). But it took a whole year for the monks to make good their claim: repairs to the bridge had been completed on 18 October 1361.

17 In the 1343 report (Appendix 2, no. 5) the name *Westerham* is written between the lines: purposely or otherwise, it came close to being omitted.

18 The individual figures quoted are as follows: for a derelict area adjoining the eastern bridgehead, £13 6s 8d; for span 1, £93 6s 8d; for span 2, £5; for span 3, £10; for span 4, £120; for span 5, £80; for span 6, £60; for spans 7 and 8, £66 13s 4d; for span 9, £26; for the barbican, no figure; for the western bridgehead, £60. Not counting the barbican, the total works out at £534 6s 8d, as was reported by Hasted (1782, p. 17, note f).

19 In 1391 the builders of the new bridge asserted that the places responsible for repairing the old bridge had been 'very nearly ruined and reduced to nothing (*bien pres destruitz et anientez*)' by the cost they had to carry (*Rotuli parliamentorum*, vol. 3, p. 290). But petitions of this kind were always hyperbolic, exaggerating both the defects of the existing situation and the advantages to be looked for from some proposed improvement. The motive here was to persuade the king that the old bridge should be abandoned, and that the traditional arrangement would not suffice for the maintenance of the new bridge.

20 The commissioners appointed on 10 February 1355 were instructed to ascertain 'the names ... of those who have received any moneys for the repair and have not laid them out in such repair and to compel, or, if need be, distrain ... those who have received money as above to apply the same to the repairs' (*Calendar of patent rolls 1354-8*, p. 230). After that a clause of this type becomes common form.

21 *Rotuli parliamentorum*, vol. 3, pp. 289-90. The arrangement is said to have existed 'from time immemorial (*de temps dont memorie ne court*)', but that should not be taken too literally.

22 *Calendar of patent rolls 1307-13*, p. 348. The men named are Simon Potyn of Rochester and Robert de Bettlescumbe. Potin was the name of a family established in the city since before 1200: Simon Potin was the owner of the Crown Inn and the founder of St Katherine's hospital in Eastgate. Robert de Betlescumbe was also a local man, but I do not know much about him, except that he represented Rochester in Parliament several times.

23 Most notably, successive heads of the de Cobham family − John (d. 1300), Henry (d. 1339), John (d. 1355), John (d. 1408) − were largely immune from contributing to the bridge. (For details of the land they held, see, for example, *Calendar of inquisitions post mortem 1405-13*, pp. 124-5.) Their manors of Cooling, Cobham, and Beckley, though well within the catchment, for one reason or another were not included in the

bridgework text. Two small manors, Pool and Bromhey, were held from the bishop of Rochester: they both originated as portions carved out of the church's manors to support the bishop's knights. It is possible that these were required to contribute along with the parent manors of Southfleet and Frindsbury, like the similar holdings in Wouldham (above, p. 8, note 24); but the indications are that they were not.

24 From the letter cited in the next note, we discover that Simon de Creye (not 'Greye'), 'when he had the custody of the castle and town during the disturbance in the realm', refused to pay the monks of Rochester any share of the takings from the ferry. Creye took charge of the castle and city some time after the siege of April 1264, some time before January 1267; the exact date does not seem to be recorded, but evidently the bridge was still out of action when he first arrived.

25 On 15 April 1282 the king ordered John de Cobham − as 'keeper of the castle and town of Rochester' − to ensure that the prior and convent of Rochester were given 'the fourth penny from the ferry over the water there'; he was to see to it that they got their share of the money received 'since the breaking of the bridge', including the arrears previously withheld from them (*Calendar of close rolls 1279-88*, pp. 152-3).

26 A grant of the profits from the ferry 'until the bridge, now broken, shall be repaired' was issued on 17 June 1310 (*Calendar of patent rolls 1307-13*, pp. 232, 233; cf. *Calendar of Chancery warrants*, p. 333). An undignified dispute involving the king's bailiff, two men of Westerham, one horse, and five cows (*Calendar of inquisitions miscellaneous (Chancery)*, vol. 2, p. 26) proves that span 5 was under repair in 1310-11. A more dignified difference of opinion involving the king, the sheriff, and a local landowner, Geoffrey de Say (*Calendar of close rolls 1307-13*, p. 347), proves the same for at least one other span. Two of the manors held by this man (*Calendar of inquisitions post mortem 1316-27*, pp. 191-2) occur in the bridgework text, Burham (span 4) and Birling (span 9); so one or other or both of these spans must also have been repaired.

27 Brooks says that 'the bridge was broken' on 'no fewer than nineteen occasions between 1277 and 1381', and that 'the bridge was broken almost annually' in the mid fourteenth century (1994, pp. 38, 39). But that is to assume that the bridge was broken on every occasion when we find it mentioned in the records of central government. In fact, between 1340 and 1381, though the bridge is mentioned frequently, there is no suggestion that it ever collapsed, only that it was often in need of repair.

28 This is Brooks's idea (1994, p. 40): he thinks that the stone supports may have started to give way. But his reading of the evidence is compromised, here and elsewhere, by the mistranslation of *pera* as 'pier'. In November 1391 the builders of the new stone bridge were trying to persuade the king that the old bridge ought to be abandoned, and that the places which had been responsible for its repair should now be made responsible for the upkeep of the new bridge (*Rotuli parliamentorum*, vol. 3, pp. 289-90). By their account, the old bridge, 'because of the great depth of the salt water ... and the roughness of the waves', was 'very nearly destroyed, without hope of its being rebuilt (*bien pres destruitz, sanz espoier ou relevation d'icell*)'. But that is just more hyperbole (above, note 19).

29 The two men appointed to act as 'keepers of the bridge of Rochester' in 1311 (above, note 22) were ordered to address this problem.

4
Oblivion

At the beginning of February 1381 the bridge was broken again, for what turned out to be the final time. The damage is said to have been caused 'by inundations of the Medeweye';[1] more circumstantially, a chronicler tells us that a great shelf of ice had developed on the upstream side of the bridge, that when the weather changed this shelf broke up, and that the detached masses of ice, in forcing their way through the bridge, destroyed 'a large part' of the structure.[2]

As on previous occasions, the first thought was to organize a ferry. In May the king issued a letter (valid for five years) authorizing the proceeds from the ferry to be retained in Rochester and spent on repairing the bridge.[3] Already we see a departure from the usual policy. It looks as if the king's ministers, on this occasion, preoccupied with their attempts to enforce a poll-tax, were hoping to avoid the necessity of demanding yet more money from the local population; and their reluctance would doubtless have been increased by the insurrection which flared up briefly, in Kent and elsewhere, during the following month.[4] In March 1382 a commission of inquiry was appointed, with the usual instructions: to find out which people were responsible for repairing the bridge, and to compel them to get the work done.[5] If these instructions were acted upon at all, they did not achieve their purpose. A year later, the bridge was still down.

Early in 1383, a new plan was devised.[6] The first sign of this appears in February, when the king issued a letter (again valid for five years) renewing the grant he had made of the proceeds from the ferry.[7] This was superseded, five weeks later, by a similar letter (valid for seven years, 'from Easter next') dated 18 March.[8] In addition, on 20 March, the king issued a letter (likewise valid for seven years) authorizing the imposition of a special toll;[9] and from this we discover exactly what was planned. Briefly, the proposal was to build a temporary footbridge, to charge a toll on anyone using this footbridge, and to use the proceeds to help pay the cost of repairing the bridge itself. A letter of the same date authorizes two men (presumably the contractors) to impress the workmen they would need: 'stonemasons, carpenters and labourers for the works on the foot-bridge and the larger bridge over the Medeweye'.[10] As far as we know, nothing like this had ever been done before: if it had been done, we ought to know, because tolls of this kind could not be imposed without the king's authority. Over the next few months, a commission was appointed to track down any money or matériel which had been collected for the repair of the bridge but not put to its intended use;[11] and two men were licensed to collect charitable donations.[12] Thus three sources of funding were being tapped: the proceeds from the ferry, the tolls taken from people using the footbridge, and voluntary contributions. Any thought of levying the cost on the local population, as on previous occasions, seems to have been forgotten: de facto, the traditional arrangement had been allowed to lapse. After that we hear nothing more till 8 July 1387, when the king revoked his letters of 18 March 1383 (relating to the ferry) and 20 March 1383 (relating to the footbridge), both of which would otherwise have remained in force till Easter 1390.[13]

In the absence of any documentation from Rochester, it is hard to be sure what was happening on the spot. There certainly was a ferry in operation;[14] it is not so clear whether the scheme devised in March 1383 − first the construction of a footbridge,[15] then the reconstruction of the roadway − was put into execution. Important though they are, the letters recorded on the patent rolls tell us what was ordered or permitted to be done, not what was actually done. The Exchequer, for its part, had no interest in seeing the accounts. Its only direct concern was with the barbican and drawbridge at the western end of the bridge (below, p. 41), for which the king was responsible: whenever repairs were carried out here, the expenditure had to be accounted for at the Exchequer. For this reason we happen to know that some work was under way in 1385-8, under the direction of the constable;[16] and mending the drawbridge would probably have been thought a waste of money unless the rest of the bridge was also under repair.

Did the work go ahead? I see no reason not to think that it did. The silence which descends, after 1383, could mean, and in my judgement does mean, that the operations were now proceeding smoothly, without the need for further intervention from Westminster. The king's letter of 8 July 1387, cutting off the flow of funds, would then mark the moment when the repairs were completed, the ferry discontinued, the footbridge dismantled, and the bridge reopened to traffic. Instead of seven years, the repairs had been completed in not much more than four.

But there were, it seems, still some finishing touches to be applied. In November 1387 the constable of the castle and the 'keepers of the work of Roucestre bridge' were jointly given permission to take lime from the king's limekiln at Rochester, 'as much as they reasonably require for making cement', for a period of three years.[17] This appears to mean that some work still had to be done on the masonry of the barbican and western bridgehead, and that it was expected to last for a considerable length of time. Repairs to the drawbridge were indeed being carried out (and accounted for at the Exchequer) after June 1389.[18]

Meanwhile, in March 1388, for the first time, we hear of the plan to construct a new bridge – a stone bridge, not a wooden one.[19] For the next few years, the old bridge continued in use while the piers and arches of the new stone bridge took shape a short distance upstream. Construction was still in progress in November 1390;[20] twelve months later the new bridge had been completed, and arrangements for its future maintenance were being discussed.[21] Just briefly, there were two bridges in existence, side by side, rivalling one another (like the two nineteenth-century railway bridges). But the sponsors of the new bridge had little difficulty in persuading the king and his parliament that the old bridge should be abandoned, and that the places which had been responsible for repairing it should now be made responsible for maintaining the stone bridge instead. Traffic was then diverted along the new approach roads, and the old bridge was shut down for the last time. By September 1393 it was already 'so broken and decayed as to be dangerous', and a commission was appointed to decide what ought to be done to make it safe.[22] Presumably any useful timber was salvaged. The stone piers were left standing at first (below, p. 39); but in time they too disappeared.

As late as the eighteenth century, some trace of the old bridge could still be seen, when the tide was out.

The existing bridge, wrote Hasted (1782, p. 19),[23]

> is about 40 yards nearer the castle than the old one, the foundation of which is still visible at low-water, when the ground there, excepting in two narrow channels, is frequently dry.

By implication, whatever there was to see was something fairly amorphous, since otherwise the design of the old bridge would not have been (as everyone agreed it was) a matter of inference from the written sources. We shall shortly need to remember Hasted's remark, when we try to interpret certain discoveries made in 1850-51, on the line of the old bridge.

Hughes's discoveries

Whatever archaeological evidence was discovered in the 1850s, during the construction of the modern bridge and the railway bridge alongside it, was mostly destroyed or reburied without being recorded.[24] One significant discovery was described in print, not by an archaeologist, but by an engineer – a man called John Hughes.[25] Later on, some excerpts from Hughes's publication found their way into the archaeological literature; but the article needs to be read in its entirety, not in the form of disconnected quotations. It is not at all easy, from Hughes's description, to understand exactly what he had found. To make sense of what he says, we need to know something about the circumstances.

The new bridge at Rochester was designed by William Cubitt. Not counting the movable section on the Strood side, the bridge was planned to consist of three cast-iron spans supported by stone piers and abutments. To carry the stonework, arrays of piles were to be sunk into the bed of the river: fourteen for either pier (Fig. 6), twelve for the abutment on the Rochester side, thirty for the Strood abutment. The piles were to be assembled on the spot from prefabricated components – cast-iron cylinders 9 feet long and either 6 feet or 7 feet in diameter (6 feet for the abutments, 7 feet for the piers). Once the piles were in position, the spaces inside them were to be packed with concrete and brickwork.

John Hughes, an employee of Cubitt's, was put in charge of this phase of the construction. When he arrived on the site, he was intending to use a method which had been tried before elsewhere, and which worked well enough if the riverbed consisted of loose alluvial deposits, as was assumed to be the case at Rochester. But that assumption promptly turned out

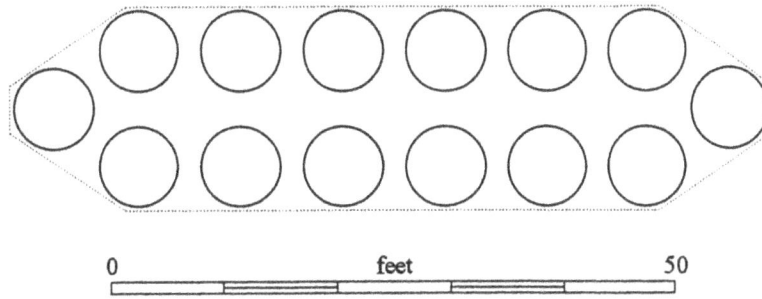

Fig. 6. The arrangement of piles supporting the Strood pier
of the modern bridge.

to be false. As soon as he started work, beginning with the (so-called) Strood pier (which in fact stands almost in the middle of the river), Hughes hit an obstacle. Instead of soft clay or sand, the bed of the river proved to consist of 'a mass of hard rock, or stone, closely packed together'. Shortly afterwards, taking advantage of 'an unusually low tide', he was able to walk down and take a close look at the problem. Beneath a few inches of mud, the whole space where the piles needed to be sunk was occupied by 'a compact mass of Kentish rag-stone, of a thickness that could not readily be ascertained'.[26] This means that the rubble mass was continuous over an area roughly 70 feet long by 20 feet wide, extending beyond these limits in every direction.

Faced with this unexpected difficulty, Hughes had to improvise. The method he devised involved sealing the pile at the top and pumping air into it until the pressure was high enough for the water to be expelled. Entering through an airlock, the workmen climbed down to the bottom of the pile, where they hacked away the rubble from beneath their feet, to the depth of a foot or two. That done, they climbed up again and exited through the airlock. Then the pressure was released, and the pile sank a little deeper, under its own weight. (At this point, whenever it became necessary, another cylinder could be added to the top of the pile.) The whole process was then repeated, over and over again, till finally the base of the pile was lodged in solid chalk. After that, the apparatus could be rigged up again, in the position required for the next pile. Thanks to Hughes's ingenuity – and thanks to heroic efforts by the labourers, who kept working round the clock, by candlelight, in this constricted and pressurized environment – the fourteen piles for the Strood pier were all successfully completed.

At this stage of the work, Hughes wrote a paper describing the method which he had invented; and in May 1851 the paper was read at a meeting of the Institution of Civil Engineers. (The meeting was chaired by Cubitt, the Institution's president at the time.) The discussion which followed was mainly concerned with the engineering aspects of the paper, but some of the people present showed an interest in the archaeology too. Asked for further details, Hughes replied by giving the following account of the stratigraphy:

The first 15 feet consisted of rubble-stone, and large pieces of timber were sometimes found right across the cylinder; the next 8 feet were of gravel; then 3 feet of soft chalk, and lastly, a bed of hard chalk.[27]

That is clear enough, as far as it goes.

Hughes's paper was published straight away, with a transcript of the discussion, in the *Minutes of proceedings* issued to the Institution's members.[28] There is a paragraph appearing in the printed text which sounds to me as if it was inserted later, after the paper had been read, in response to the questions raised by members of the audience. What Hughes says here is this:

a mass of Kentish rag-stone, of the nature of rubble without mortar, is found for a depth varying from 13 feet to 25 feet below the present bed of the river. Pieces of timber of considerable dimensions, and which had been used as piles, or framing, occurred in this bed of rubble-stone, penetrating a foot, or two into the gravel, which proved to be 6 feet, or 8 feet thick. This timber is oak, elm, and beech, – all, except the last, perfectly sound and tough (a few pieces had evidently been burnt); the beech was saturated with water, and was in the condition of a soft pulp. Some fragments of iron proved, that the piles had been shod with that material (p. 365).

This seems to be a jumble of half-remembered (or half-forgotten) facts, to which at the time – having

33

more important things on his mind – he had paid no particular attention, but which now appeared to be of interest to other people.

Hughes had also got hold of a copy of Fisher's *History*. Using that source alone, he summarized what was known (or supposed to be known) about the earliest recorded bridge at Rochester. Seen in that light, the evidence which he had found now seemed to him to have 'established the fact' that the Strood pier of the new bridge 'occupies the site of one of the piers which carried the wooden bridge'. The idea that he had found the footing for a pier seems to have originated as a casual suggestion by somebody else, during the discussion of his paper; but Hughes adopted it and took it to mean that each of the ancient piers had a separate footing, one of which happened to coincide, almost exactly, with the modern pier. This interpretation is doubtful, and, by my reckoning, has only a low probability of being right.[29] There is an alternative, viz. that the rubble formed a continuous shelf across the whole width of the river. All that Hughes had found, I suspect, was an unstructured mass of ballast, dumped here from time to time, around and between the piers of the bridge, to counteract erosion of the river-bed. At any rate, that is the hypothesis I think we ought to prefer, until we have some decisive evidence one way or the other.[30]

However that may be, it is certainly true that Hughes's paper was written, read, and published at a time when the work at Rochester was still in progress.[31] He talks about the Strood pier because that is where the engineering difficulty was first encountered, and where it was first successfully overcome. This paper cannot tell us what was or was not found under the other pier, or under either abutment. To let us know that, Hughes would have had to write a sequel, and this he did not do.[32] But since it was clearly his intention to keep on using the same method, there is some reason to think that he expected to keep on colliding with the same sort of obstacle.

NOTES

1 *Calendar of patent rolls 1381-5*, p. 5 (14 May 1381).

2 *Isto anno circa Purificacionem beate Marie dirupta fuit magna pars pontis Roucestr'; fuerat quidem glacies inmensa, que postmodum tepido aere resoluta mole suarum parcium ponti incumbencium pontem confregit* (from a chronicle written at Westminster, ed. Hector and Harvey 1982, p. 2). What happened, I suppose, was something similar to what is

recorded in 1799 (Ormrod 1994, p. 206). Another contemporary chronicler – unidentified, but well informed about Kentish matters – reports that 'a great mass of ice (*magna glacies*) struck the wooden bridge of Rochester and broke it, so that a ferry was in operation there for a long time' (ed. Haydon 1858-63, vol. 3, p. 351).

3 *Calendar of patent rolls 1381-5*, p. 5 (14 May 1381); as noted by Britnell (1994, p. 43, note 4), in this context the word *feria* means 'ferry', not 'fair'. All three of the men named here – William Basynge (master of Strood hospital), Nicholas Heryng, Sir Robert de Assheton – died within the next few years: Basynge by August 1383, Heryng by February 1383, Assheton by January 1384. A high death-rate among the people involved seems to be one of the contingent reasons which delayed the repair of the bridge.

4 In June 1381 the castle at Rochester underwent its last and least glorious siege. The constable, Sir John de Newenton, surrendered to the rebels after a few hours.

5 *Calendar of patent rolls 1381-5*, p. 136 (20 March 1382).

6 Without wishing to seem perverse, I read the evidence differently from Brooks (1994, p. 40), who thinks that the old bridge was left unrepaired after 1381, and differently again from Britnell (1994, p. 44), who thinks that a new bridge was already being planned in 1383. It seems to me that the old bridge was repaired, and that the thought of building a new bridge did not become a serious proposition till 1388. The whole sequence of events should probably be reconsidered, by somebody who (unlike me) enjoys easy access to the Public Record Office.

7 *Calendar of patent rolls 1381-5*, p. 221 (12 February 1383). Nicholas Heryng, 'now deceased', was replaced by Robert Rowe, whose involvement with the bridge was to last for more than thirty years (Britnell 1994, pp. 58-9). At the supervisory level, Assheton was replaced by a panel of four: Sir John de Cobham, Sir John Philipot, Sir John de Newenton, and master Henry Yevele. By the way, there is no evidence connecting Yevele with the construction of the new bridge, only with the repair of the old one.

8 *Calendar of patent rolls 1381-5*, p. 235 (18 March 1383). There are two other versions of this letter (ibid. pp. 240, 241), seemingly later, though with the same nominal date. They both substitute the name of Sir Simon de Burley for that of Sir John Philipot. Philipot was still on the panel in August 1383, still alive in April 1384, dead by November 1384; Burley by then had been appointed to take his place (ibid. pp. 308, 506). The third version, which adds a clause to the effect that no auditing of the accounts is required, seems for that reason to be later than June 1385 (below, note 14).

9 *Calendar of patent rolls 1381-5*, p. 243 (20 March 1383). The grant was renewed on 26 August (ibid. p. 308), because Basynge had died meanwhile. He was replaced by Thomas Brumlegh (his successor also as master of Strood hospital).

10 *Calendar of patent rolls 1381-5*, p. 239 (20 March 1383). As I understand this, the larger bridge is simply the existing bridge, called 'larger' to distinguish it from the temporary footbridge.

11 *Calendar of patent rolls 1381-5*, p. 262 (7 April 1383).

12 *Calendar of patent rolls 1381-5*, p. 273 (14 May 1383),

p. 275 (10 June 1383).

13 *Calendar of patent rolls 1385-9*, p. 328 (8 July 1387).

14 On two occasions commissioners were appointed to audit the accounts of the proceeds from the ferry: *Calendar of patent rolls 1381-5*, p. 506 (17 November 1384), *Calendar of patent rolls 1385-9*, p. 79 (29 June 1385). In the event, neither of these letters was acted on: in both cases a note has been added to the roll saying that 'nothing was done' (apparently because it was decided that the accounts could be handled by the supervisory panel – Cobham, Burley, Newenton, Yevele – without independent auditors (above, note 8)). Nevertheless they go to prove that money from the ferry had begun to be collected before February 1383, was still being collected, and was expected to continue being collected at least till 4 July 1385.

15 The footbridge, I suppose, was a wooden gangway, only a few feet wide, perched on the (downstream?) extremities of the piers of the existing bridge, where it would not interfere with the reconstruction of the roadway. As well as pedestrians, horses were allowed to cross, but they had to be led, not ridden. Vehicles presumably continued to use the ferry.

16 *Lists and indexes*, vol. 11, p. 119, from the foreign account rolls for 8 and 10 Richard II.

17 *Calendar of patent rolls 1385-9*, p. 377 (27 November 1387).

18 *Lists and indexes*, vol. 11, p. 119, from the foreign account roll for 12 Richard II.

19 *Calendar of patent rolls 1385-9*, p. 416 (18 March 1388). Sir Robert Knolles now makes his first appearance, as one of the promoters of the plan for a new bridge, in partnership with John de Cobham (Britnell 1994, pp. 45-7). As far as we can judge, Cobham supplied the inspiration and Knolles supplied the money. Knolles died in 1407, Cobham in 1408; so they were both spared from knowing that in 1409, only eighteen years after its completion, the stone bridge would suffer the first of a series of disasters caused by structural failure.

20 *Calendar of patent rolls 1388-92*, p. 316 (22 October 1390), p. 329 (25 November 1390).

21 Knolles and Cobham submitted their petition to the king in November 1391 (*Rotuli parliamentorum*, vol. 3, pp. 289-90).

22 *Calendar of patent rolls 1391-6*, pp. 357, 358 (18 September 1393).

23 This is partly based on a remark in Fisher's *History* (1772, p. 50, note): 'The foundation of the old bridge is still visible at low water, in spring tides, the ground there being frequently dry'.

24 If Charles Roach Smith had moved to Strood a few years sooner than he did, we might have been better informed; but that is an idle regret.

25 I know scarcely anything about him, beyond what can be inferred from this paper (Hughes 1851), which seems to be the only article he ever published. (He was awarded a prize for it in the following year.) The pneumatic caisson method, pioneered by Hughes at Rochester, became part of the normal repertoire of engineering techniques.

26 These quotations come from Hughes's introductory remarks (1851, p. 356), which are straightforward reportage, unbiased by any attempt at interpretation.

27 This is Hughes's impromptu reply, as quoted in *Minutes of proceedings of the Institution of Civil Engineers*, x (1851), 367. Hughes does not say – and probably did not think to ask – whether the layer of gravel was a geological or an archaeological layer. I guess that it was geological.

28 The copy of this volume which I have used (the copy in the University of Birmingham library) is a reprint containing a few notes added by the editor, Charles Manby, in 1857. These notes are significant in one respect (below, note 31), but they do not touch on archaeological matters.

29 Suppose that we drop a modern pier onto a line of ancient piers. If we assume the modern pier to be narrower than the ancient piers, there are three possible outcomes: (1) our pier misses the ancient piers, falling into one of the spaces between them; (2) our pier hits the edge of one of the ancient piers; (3) our pier hits one of the ancient piers so nearly in the centre that neither of its edges is revealed. *Ex hypothesi* we do not know the width of the ancient piers, nor the width of the intervening spaces; but if we estimate those dimensions, we can associate probabilities with the various outcomes. On any reasonable estimates, outcome (3) is the least likely.

30 Brooks (1994, pp. 10-11) reports using 'an extendable aluminium probe' to explore the riverbed beneath the bridge, from a motor launch. The bottom, he says, 'does not consist of the thick alluvial mud that is general in the Medway estuary, but has a compacted hard surface of stone or brick'; he suggests that this material was deposited 'when the bridge was built in the 1850s or else during its reconstruction of 1908-11'. I see no reason why the 'compacted hard surface' struck by Brooks's probe should not be the same as the 'mass of hard rock, or stone, closely packed together' encountered by Hughes's workmen.

31 This is clear, for instance, from the fact that Hughes is reported as saying that 'the works were conducted, at present, under a pressure of 44 feet of water, but they were prepared for sustaining a pressure of 62 feet 6 inches' (*Minutes of proceedings*, p. 367). At the foot of this page is one of the comments added later by Manby (above, note 28): 'Before the works at Rochester were completed, the column of water was 61 feet'.

32 Wheeler (1932, p. 85) pointed out that there is a passage in Smiles's *Lives of the engineers* (1874-9, vol. 2, p. 44) asserting that something was found during the construction of the railway bridge. I doubt whether this was anything more than a misremembered reference to Hughes's paper.

5

Reconstruction

When Lambarde put some of this written evidence into print for the first time, he said nothing much about its structural significance, except to note the obvious point (obvious to him) that the bridge consisted of nine spans – 'nine Arches, or peres' (above, p. 6). But the quantity of information contained in these and other documents is enough to encourage the hope that we may be able to reconstruct the bridge – in the mind's eye, or on paper (or, better still, as a model) – in rather more detail than that.

Any attempt to reconstruct the bridge is bound to involve some guesswork. In a sense, the whole enterprise is guesswork. It is only worth trying so far as we have some means of deciding whether one guess is better or worse than another. There seem to be three criteria available to us. First, the reconstruction has to be in satisfactory agreement with the documentary evidence. Second, it has to fit the topography of the site; and this means, for a start, that the bridge has to be long enough to reach from one side of the river to the other. Third, it has to be structurally sound: the bridge has to be strong enough to last for some considerable period of time, carrying some considerable weight of traffic. A guess is only a good guess if it is good in all three respects.

A reconstruction which satisfies the third criterion was worked out and published in the 1780s. Then as now, archaeologists were mostly ignorant of engineering; then as now, they sometimes had the sense to consult the advice of an expert. James Essex, who not only had practical experience of building bridges but also knew more than anybody else about medieval architecture,[1] was invited to give some thought to the documents printed by Lambarde; and he produced a paper explaining (not very clearly) how he interpreted the evidence, and how he had arrived at a reconstruction of the bridge.

Essex's reconstruction

The circumstances in which Essex's paper came to be written are revealed by some of the correspondence published in Nichols's *Literary illustrations* (1831).[2] Essex started thinking about this problem, not on his own initiative, but because he was asked to do so, by Richard Gough; Gough was thinking about it because he too had been asked to, by Samuel Denne; and Denne was thinking about it because he had promised to help in preparing a new edition of Fisher's *History of Rochester*.

Thomas Fisher was a bookseller in Rochester who set up his own printing-press in 1770. One of his more ambitious productions was a guidebook called *The history and antiquities of Rochester and its environs*, published in 1772. Several authors, all anonymous, contributed portions of the text. One of them was Samuel Denne, who wrote the chapter about the history of the medieval priory.[3] Somebody else – we do not know who – drew up an account of the old bridge, based on the documents printed in Harris's *History of Kent*. This is a feeble piece of work, with nothing much to be said in its favour except that it was indeed the first published attempt to make some structural sense of the documentary evidence.[4]

A second edition of Fisher's *History* – to be published in two volumes, with considerable additions – was advertised in 1783 (Rye 1887, p. 67), though in the event it never saw the light. Once again, Denne was involved in the project. Writing to Gough in August that year,[5] he reproaches him (Gough) for having failed to visit him (Denne) while travelling recently through Kent. He goes on:

Possibly when you was at Rochester you saw Mr Fisher, and if you did he doubtless told you of his intention to publish a new edition of the History and Antiquities of that place, &c. My partiality for a place where I so long lived has drawn me in to promise to revise and enlarge the work; but I find myself engaged in a more arduous task than I expected, especially as I cannot in my country retirement have several books I wish to consult.

Then he raises the question of the bridge:

The description given of the old timber bridge in the present edition does not by any means satisfy me. After a careful perusal of the MSS in the Textus Roffensis,[6] relative to the repair of it, I am clear that the person whom Fisher employed to write that chapter was mistaken in his idea of the piers being placed at equal distances from one another.

Denne preferred to think that the measurements of planking corresponded with the distances between the piers, which on this view would vary greatly from span to span. But if the unit of measurement was assumed to be a standard rod of 16½ feet, the longest span would be 66 feet across, and this seemed hard to credit:

I cannot conceive how sylle (rendered by the writer beams) could be found of a sufficient length and bulk to support the weight of the planks, and of the heavy burdens which were to be carried over the bridge.

The wording here echoes the additional paragraph found in the Latin version of the bridgework text.

Gough sought expert advice. For help in understanding the wording of the text he wrote to Owen Manning (above, p. 6). Manning replied,[7] beginning his letter with the comment quoted above, pointing out that *per* did not mean 'pier' but 'span'. Then he answered the queries put to him by Gough. Since he understood Gough to have said that the river at Rochester was 431 feet wide,[8] he thought it reasonable to assume that a *gyrd* was the same as a rod. The word *syll*, he explained, meant 'a large piece of timber hewn square': he suggested that the 'sylles' were 'joists which lay across the bridge from side to side, to which the planking was nailed'.

For advice on the engineering aspects of the problem, Gough consulted Essex − not only the person best qualified but also a friend. He wrote to Essex (who lived in Cambridge) asking him to look at the texts printed by Lambarde, to see how much sense he could make of them. Essex reported his first thoughts on the subject in a letter dated 22 September:[9]

I have examined Lambarde's account of Rochester bridge, but find a difficulty in understanding him. The manuscript from which he has taken the account is curious, but does not contain particulars sufficient to give an idea of the structure of the bridge; it only mentions the works that were to be done by particular people. All I can collect from it is, that the bridge consisted of nine piers, which I suppose were built with timber (but of this I cannot be certain); it had eight arches or passages, over which the sylls were laid from pier to pier, and on them the planks which formed the floor of the bridge. The whole length was 26 yards,[10] or rather poles, equal to 429 feet, including the abutments; these, I suppose, were about 30 feet each, the seven piers about 16 feet each, and the arches about 32 feet each, the breadth of the bridge about 17 feet clear, except over the two middle arches, which I believe were wider by three or four feet. The number of sylls or beams, which were about 40 feet long, was 90 or upwards; 28 of these, with about 26 rods of planking, belonged to those who built or repaired the nine piers, the rest to those who made or repaired the railing on both sides.

It seems clear that Essex was never made aware of Manning's suggestion that *per* meant 'span'. He did notice that Lambarde treated 'pere' and 'arch' as synonyms; but he assumed that this was a blunder. The bridge envisaged by Essex had nine supports − two abutments plus seven free-standing piers − and therefore it had eight openings. He also assumed, straight away, that the deck consisted of transverse planking carried by longitudinal beams.

A second letter, dated 8 November,[11] makes it clear that Gough had been pressing for more information, and for a drawing; he also wanted authorization for Denne to make use of Essex's previous remarks. Essex wrote:

I will take an early opportunity to make a plan of Rochester bridge; but, as my last observations were made in haste, I will examine the account of it in Lambarde with more attention. When I have made that clear to myself, I will send you my thoughts upon it; until then I wish Mr Denne not to make any use of what I sent before.

Some time later he wrote out a draft of his paper and sent it to Gough;[12] and Gough forwarded it to Denne on 26 December, saying that he could keep it as long as he liked.

Denne kept it for more than three months. On 16 April he wrote to Gough,[13] with thanks for the loan of the paper, and apologies for the delay in returning it. He is 'perfectly satisfied', he says, 'of the justness of the greater part' of Essex's observations; and he concedes it to be most likely 'that such doubts as I may have remaining proceed from my having no skill in architecture'. From the published version of this letter it is not clear what these doubts were, or what comments, if any, Denne made. But certainly some further queries were put to Essex by Gough, because Essex apologizes, in a letter dated 3 May,[14] for not being well enough to answer them. He died a few months later, on 14 September 1784.

His paper was read at a meeting of the Society of Antiquaries on 17 March 1785, and published shortly afterwards, in the seventh volume of *Archaeologia*, with a plate engraved (by James Basire) from Essex's drawing, showing the bridge in plan and elevation. Presumably Denne would have wanted to comment on this reconstruction, in the second edition of Fisher's *History*; but that project lapsed with Fisher's death in the following year.

As Essex imagined it, the bridge consisted of eight spans carried by nine supports − seven free-standing piers and an abutment at either end (Fig. 7). He took

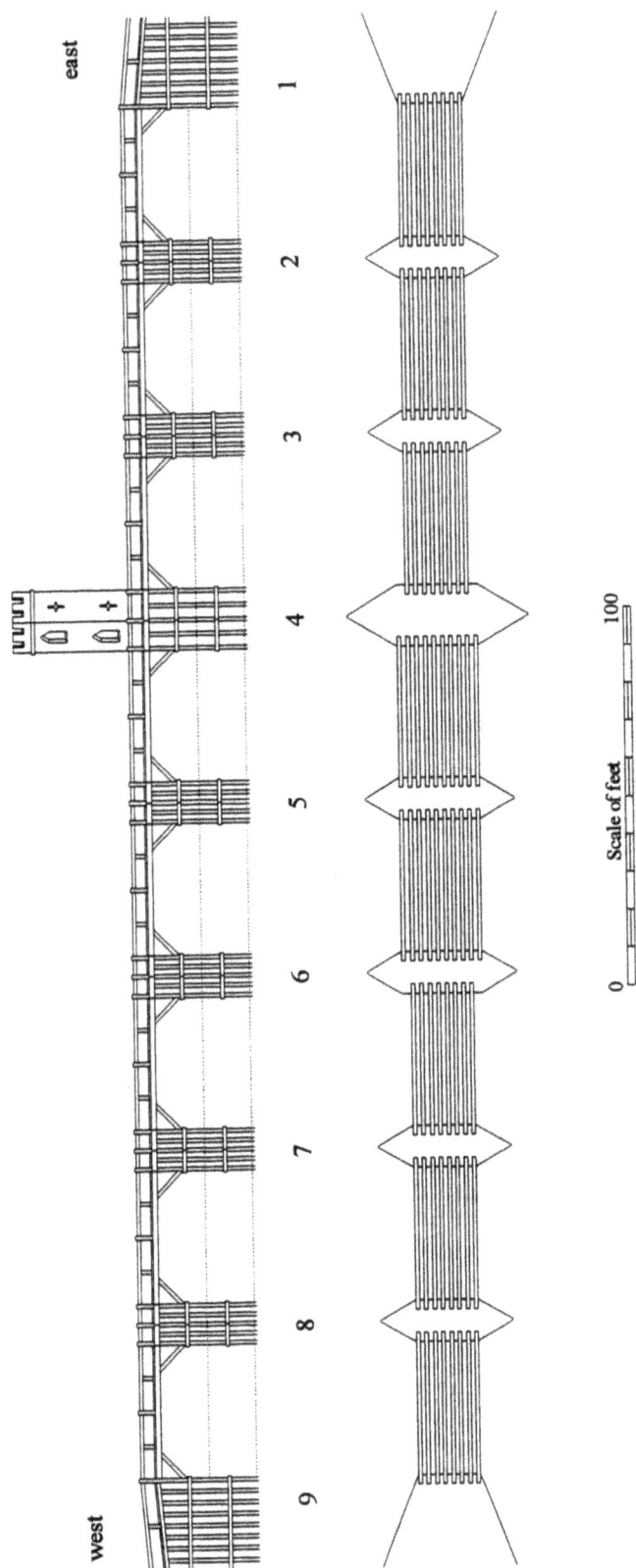

Fig. 7. The bridge as reconstructed by Essex (1785).

it for granted that the spans would all be equal, without seeing any need to explain his reasons; for each he reckoned on a length of 35 feet. The piers, he guessed, were wooden structures, timber frameworks packed with rubble. For each he allowed a width of 11 feet, though the pier which carried the hypothetical tower (see below) might, he thought, have been larger than the rest. Allowing 16 feet for this larger pier, and assuming an overlap of 20 feet between the wooden roadway and the abutment at either end, he calculated the overall length of the bridge as 402 feet. Measured between the abutments, however, the length is only 362 feet.

At first sight, perhaps, Essex's bridge has a rather quaint appearance, reminiscent of the sort of rustic bridge which an eighteenth-century architect might have built in the grounds of some stately home, for a patron with a taste for the picturesque. But we need to concentrate on the basic design, not letting ourselves be distracted by details which were only added as finishing touches. Essex was a trained carpenter and builder, as well as an architect: he knew how to put together a wooden bridge. Some features of his reconstruction are discussed below, but I think we can take it as given, straight away, that a bridge built to Essex's design would be sufficiently strong.

In the middle of Essex's bridge, on top of the fourth pier (the 'pier' which belonged to the king), there is a tower. West of the tower, for the length of two spans, the roadway is somewhat broader than elsewhere, the idea being, as Essex explains, that this would give the defenders the advantage of having more room for manoeuvre. Apparently from the outset, he assumed that the bridge ought to be provided with fortifications. Though he does not specifically mention this analogy, he seems to have visualized the bridge at Rochester as a wooden version of the (thirteenth-century) fortified bridge at Monmouth. Curiously, the defences are back to front. Essex had visited Rochester more than once, but on this occasion (sitting at his desk in Cambridge) he seems to have got it into his head that the city was on the west bank;[15] so the tower faces towards the east, and the advantage intended to be conferred on the defenders is in fact conferred on the attackers.

This tower, though it catches the eye, is not of much significance. We can dispose of it quickly, and may as well do so at once. During the civil wars of the 1260s, the dissident barons, in April 1264, attempted to capture Rochester. Earl Simon, arriving from the west, began with an attack on the bridge. A report of this battle, written by one of the Rochester monks,[16] informs us that there were fortifications of some kind built upon the bridge (*propugnacula superedificata*). Since they are said to have been burnt, they were presumably of wood; since they are said to have been constructed 'with wondrous skill' *(mirabili artis ingenio)*, they must have been something more than improvised barricades. Essex's tower seems to have been based on this evidence, so far as it was based on anything. But we do not know what exactly these fortifications consisted of, nor where exactly they were placed. In any case, they seem to have been temporary structures, erected only two years before,[17] not a permanent feature of the design.

A new reconstruction

To work out a new reconstruction of the bridge, the wisest policy, it seems to me, is to start with Essex's design, and to ask what improvements we can make. This policy was not my first choice. On the contrary, I began with the assumption that starting from scratch would be best. A picture of the bridge would emerge, I thought, if I forced myself to look hard enough at the written evidence. But that policy failed, and kept on failing, until in the end I realized that Essex is the most trustworthy guide we can find.

There are two improvements we can make without hesitation: we can remove Essex's fortifications, which serve only to confuse the issue; and we can agree with Lambarde and Manning that the bridge consisted of nine spans, not eight (above, pp. 5-6). A third improvement is almost as quickly made: we can substitute stone piers for the wooden structures which Essex felt obliged to make do with. From evidence unknown to him, it happens to be fairly certain that the piers were built of stone. The evidence comes from the Bridge Wardens' account rolls — that is, the sequence of financial statements, beginning in 1398, produced annually by the custodians of the newly completed bridge, and still preserved at Rochester (Becker 1930, Scroggs 1954). From some of the entries in these accounts, it becomes clear that the abandoned bridge was not demolished straight away. The piers remained in place, downstream from the new bridge; and when stone was needed for making repairs to the latter, some of it was obtained by robbing the derelict structure. Mostly the stone procured in this way was rubble, but on one occasion cut stone is mentioned too (Becker 1930, p. 74; Britnell 1994, p. 67). With stone piers, and with an extra span, our bridge is already longer and stronger than Essex's.

A glance at the topography (Fig. 1) is enough to show that we need to make the bridge as long as we possibly can, without compromising the strength of the design. In Essex's bridge, the spans are of 35 feet; and he warns us, by implication, not to try stretching them further, for it is likely that he would himself have preferred to make the spans larger, had he thought it safe to do so. For example, with 40-foot spans and 16-foot piers, his bridge would have been $8 \times 40 + 7 \times 16 = 432$ feet long, almost exactly the length required on what Essex would have thought to be the simplest reading of the evidence — i.e. that the bridge was 26½ rods long (the figure obtained by adding up the specified quantities of planking). His first guess was that the spans would be about 32 feet across (above, p. 37); he increased this on second thoughts, but only by 3 feet.

There are several considerations which come into play here. The beams which Essex had in mind were single pieces of oak, each of them 40 feet long and 12 inches square. He was willing to assume (tacitly) that it would have been possible for beams of this size to be procured, not just when the bridge was first built, but also whenever some part of it needed repair. If we think of making the beams much larger than that, we shall have to start questioning this assumption.[18] Then there is the question of weight. At its densest, oak can weigh as much as 60 pounds per cubic foot, so Essex's beams would each weigh around 1 ton. He was willing to assume (again tacitly) that the engineers responsible for building the bridge and for maintaining it later would have had the machinery available to them for handling beams of this weight. If we think of using much heavier beams, we cannot rely on Essex's experience to justify this assumption. Third, and most important, there are the constraints imposed by the elasticity of timber. No one needs to be told that a wooden beam will bend, when it is put under a load; but it may be a surprise to learn that the deflection of a beam increases (other things being equal) with the fourth power of its length.[19] For this reason, as I said before (above, p. 25), the design of a wooden deck depends very sensitively on the length of the span; and that is why Essex took it for granted that the spans would all be equal, or very nearly so.[20]

On the other hand, we can hardly think of reducing the size of the spans by any significant margin. With nine spans of 35 feet, the bridge has a waterway of

$9 \times 35 = 315$ feet. This is similar to the waterway of the medieval bridge, which had eleven openings averaging about 30 feet each.[21] But the design of the medieval bridge was barely adequate to cope with the volume of water flowing through it (Ormrod 1994, p. 170). Having two fewer spans to work with, we need to make them as large as we possibly can, so as to maximize the waterway.

In short, we do not seem to have much choice in the matter. Essex effectively tells us that a span of 35 feet is the maximum span that he would be willing to build, using wooden frames to carry the deck; and we do best to take his word for it. If he had known that the piers were built of stone, perhaps he might have been willing to stretch the spans a little more; but I doubt whether this would have made a significant difference.

With regard to the piers, we are not so tightly restricted. The 11-foot piers envisaged by Essex are relatively slender structures, not even one-third as wide as the width of the spans. Given that the piers were of stone, I would be ready to guess that they were proportionally much more massive than Essex thought. If we agree that the spans may have been as much as 36 feet across, it does not seem unreasonable to think that the piers may have been as much as 24 feet across, i.e. two-thirds as much.[22] That would give us a bridge with an overall length of $9 \times 36 + 8 \times 24 = 516$ feet, measured between the abutments. To make the bridge any longer than that seems practically impossible.

The bridge as we reconstruct it, though appreciably longer than Essex's bridge, is still not long enough to reach across the whole width of the river. The three principal spans of the modern bridge, standing on the same site, were designed to have an overall length of about 480 feet, measured between the abutments, which is not very different from the length which we have estimated for the old bridge. But the modern bridge, as originally built,[23] had a movable section on the Strood side, so that ships too tall to pass under the three fixed spans could pass through here instead. Because of this, what is called the Strood abutment is more than 100 feet away from the waterfront on the Strood side, and what is called the Strood pier stands almost in the middle of the river. With the movable section included, the overall length of the bridge is about 620 feet between the abutments (about 650 feet from waterfront to waterfront). It follows that we have to find some way of increasing the length of our bridge, not just by some slight amount, but by over

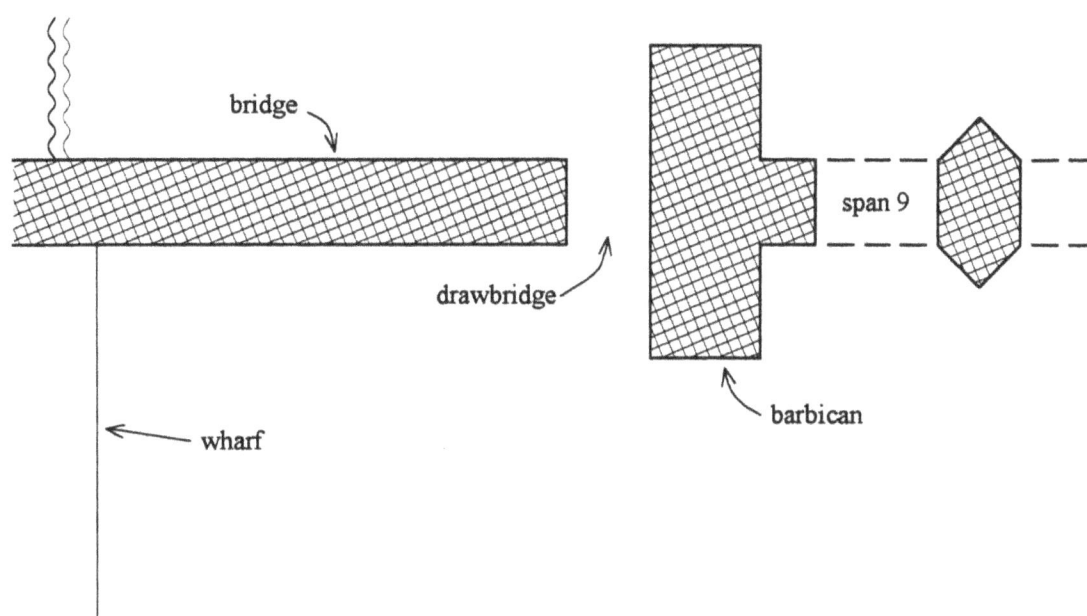

Fig. 8. A diagram showing the features associated
with the western bridgehead.

100 feet. We have already stretched the design as far
as we dare; so how can we hope to make the bridge
long enough?

To find a way out of this impasse, we need to look
again at a document mentioned already, the report
of the inquiry held at Rochester on 29 June 1343
(Appendix 2, no. 5). Basing itself, as usual, on some
version of the bridgework text, this report deals
successively with each 'pier' (i.e. span) of the bridge,
from the first to the 'ninth and last'. Thus far, there
are no surprises. But then it continues immediately
as follows:

the king makes the barbican and drawbridge; the master and
brethren of the hospital of St Mary of Strode make the bridge
with the wharf from the said drawbridge to Strode, viz. the end
of the bridge towards the west arm.

Though this may seem puzzling at first, I think the
sense of it is reasonably clear (Fig. 8). The ninth
(westernmost) span of the bridge now ends, not with
an abutment, but with a barbican – a fortified gate –
presumably built directly on top of the abutment; next
there is a drawbridge, operated from the barbican;
and then there is some further structure, itself
referred to as a 'bridge', which extends from the
drawbridge as far as the Strood side of the river.

As far as I know, there is no previous evidence
relating to the barbican. Its date is a matter of

conjecture, except that it has to be earlier than
the mid fourteenth century. One guess might be that
the fortification of the western bridgehead was part
of the general reconstruction of the city's defences
which took place in the 1220s (Flight and Harrison
1987). But the fact that wooden fortifications were
built on the bridge in 1261 seems rather to imply
that the bridge was otherwise undefended; and if that
is so the barbican would have to be regarded as a
subsequent addition. After the 1340s we know of
a few occasions when repairs to the drawbridge were
carried out, at the king's expense, by the constable
of the castle.[24] In the spring of 1388, the sheriff was
instructed to issue orders that ships, barges and boats
of every kind wanting to pass through the bridge
were all to be taken 'through the drawbridge and
through no other part of it' (*Calendar of close rolls
1385-9*, p. 482). This may mean that traffic was
being regulated with special strictness at the time,
to prevent it from interfering with the construction
of the new bridge. But in any case it seems to prove
that the barbican was surrounded by a fair depth of
water.

With regard to the 'bridge' and wharf supposed to be
kept in repair by the master and brethren of Strood
hospital, there are two earlier reports which have to
be taken into account. An inquiry held in 1276 produced a report which says – or might be thought to
say – that Strood hospital is liable for the upkeep of

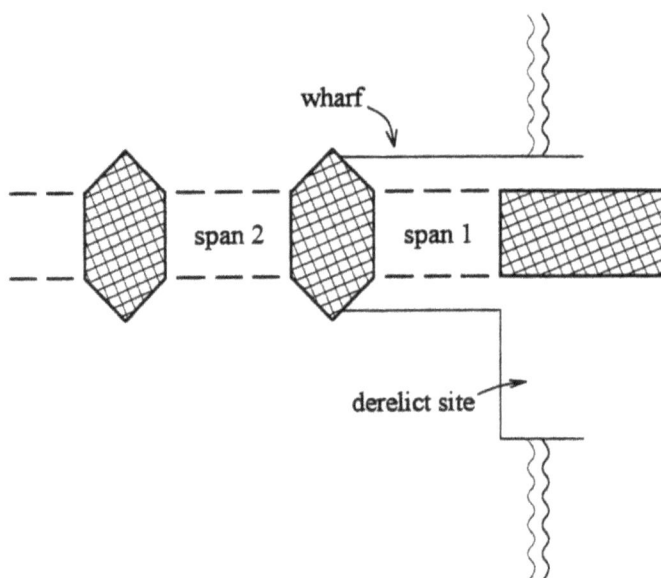

Fig. 9. A diagram showing the features associated
with the eastern bridgehead.

the whole of Rochester bridge (Appendix 2, no. 2). That must have caused some anxious moments in Strood. Strings were pulled,[25] and a second inquiry was ordered one year later. This returned a report which explains the facts more fully (Appendix 2, no. 3), though still with something less than perfect clarity. Taking all three reports together – 1276, 1277, 1343 – we can finally manage to make sense of the situation.

During the reign of king Johan, it appears, the bishop of Rochester, Gilbert de Glanville, was responsible for some redevelopment of the area adjoining the western bridgehead.[26] The scheme included a new stone wharf,[27] with buildings along it available for rent; there seems to have been a chapel too,[28] presumably next to the bridge. The rents from the buildings on the wharf became part of the endowment of the hospital of Saint Mary, founded in Strood by bishop Gilbert just a few years previously. In return, the hospital took on the responsibility for maintaining the wharf and the 'bridge' – not the whole of Rochester bridge, just the 'bridge' which formed the approach to it, from the Strood side, i.e. the 'bridge' which was also 'the end of the bridge towards the west arm'. At the time of Earl Simon's attack on Rochester (above, p. 39), some of the buildings on the wharf were set fire to by the defenders. They were still lying derelict a dozen years later, and that is why the case was inquired into.

From the fact that the approach to the bridge is called a 'bridge', I infer that it looked like a bridge.[29] What it was, I suggest, is an arched viaduct, built entirely of stone, so excluded from the remit of the bridgework text. From our point of view, the existence of this viaduct makes it easy – rather too easy – to complete our reconstruction of the bridge. In the absence of any more detailed evidence, we can vary the size of this viaduct to suit ourselves: however much additional length we need, to make our bridge fit the site, we can find it by stretching the viaduct.[30] (In the process we also obtain some extra waterway, which is welcome, though not so crucial.) If we want to add fortifications to our bridge, we can see just as easily how this is to be done: we remove the easternmost arch of the viaduct, replacing it with a drawbridge, and we build a towered gate on top of the abutment.

There was a wharf connected with the eastern bridgehead too. For understanding the structural relationships here, the most useful sources are the reports returned by the commissions of inquiry of 1343 and 1355 (Appendix 2, nos. 5-6). In the 1343 report, the wharf is explicitly equated with the first span: 'the wharf which is the first span', *warfa que est prima pera*. It seems clear, therefore, that the wharf was – in some sense, or from some point of view – coincident with this span. What had happened, I suggest, is that the space between the abutment and the first pier had been blocked off, at river level, so as to make a landing-stage for boats. In other words, there were two tiers to the structure: the roadway above, the wharf below (Fig. 9). When it speaks of 'both the woodwork and the earthwork (*tam opus ligneum quam terreum*)', the 1343 report is saying that the people responsible for this span are responsible for both tiers, not just for the timber deck.

To the south of the wharf was a patch of ground, 30 feet long, which was also causing concern. In the past, we are told, there were buildings here, and the waterfront was adequately protected. But now the buildings were gone, and the site was being eroded by the river. Exaggerating for the sake of emphasis, the report insists that the damage here ought to be made good: otherwise, however thoroughly the bridge itself were to be repaired, it would still not be safe for anybody to cross. The responsibility for making these repairs fell partly on the men of Frindsbury, partly on the city of Rochester. This was the closest the citizens came to having to pay for the upkeep of their bridge.

Putting the pieces together, I arrive at the reconstruction shown here (Fig. 10). The drawing is deliberately diagrammatic, not just to make it fit the page, but also because there is no point in pretending that we can form any clear idea of what the bridge really looked like. We see it only dimly, as if through a very thick fog. The details are all uncertain, though some are less uncertain than others; the scale is approximate, though it cannot be grossly wrong.

Carpentry

Despite the masonry which formed a large part of the structure, when people thought about the bridge at Rochester they thought of it as a wooden bridge; and of course they had a point. The structure does not become a bridge until its wooden components are put in place; it ceases to be a bridge as soon as they are removed.

What design we envisage for the wooden deck is largely a matter of guesswork. The bridgework text refers to planking and beams; the Latin version makes it clear that the beams support the planking. Presumably this means that the deck consists of transverse planking carried by longitudinal beams. In Essex's reconstruction the roadway is formed by a continuous deck of planking, with an assumed breadth of 16½-17 feet. Between the piers, the deck

is carried by timber frames, the design of which is illustrated here (Fig. 11). Essex proposed to use beams about 12 inches square, set about 15 inches apart; and he assumed that the beams would have to be supported by struts at either end.[31] For each span, this design requires twelve 40-foot-long beams: eight are to be laid horizontally from pier to pier, with an overlap of 2½ feet at either end, and the other four are to be cut into four pieces each, making eight pairs of 10-foot-long struts.

There is nothing sacrosanct about this reconstruction, which is compromised by at least one serious misunderstanding of the evidence. Essex believed that he had to contrive things so that the total number of beams was close to 100. The bridgework text supplies only 27 beams, so where did Essex think he had found the rest? One of them is the extra beam resulting from Lambarde's misprint (above, p. 4); the others were created by a misreading of the Hollingbourne memorandum, in which the responsibility for repairing two of the spans is subdivided in proportion to the number of sulungs for which each place was answerable (above, p. 4). In the text as it appears in Lambarde, the word *sulling* is never written out in full, but always shortened to *sull.* – and exactly the same abbreviation is used for *sulliua*, 'beam'. Thus, by counting up all the sulungs mentioned here, Essex thought that he had found about 70 additional beams.[32] Though that was certainly a mistake, its significance should not be overstated. What Essex tells us is this: if we are aiming to carry a roadway 17 feet wide across a span of 35 feet, a satisfactory design would consist of eight 12-inch-square beams, suitably supported by struts. We ought not to suppose that he was wrong about that, just because he did not know what the word 'sulung' meant.

The sort of design envisaged by Essex imposes no constraint on the breadth of the bridge. We could make the roadway as broad as we liked, provided we kept on adding extra beams – roughly speaking, one extra beam for each extra 2 feet of breadth. Or we could think of making it narrower, subtracting beams at the same rate. The main question, however, is whether we accept that the bridge was broad enough for traffic to pass in both directions at once. Essex took this for granted, on the grounds, I suppose, that no engineer who was capable of building a bridge this big would think it made sense to economize slightly on the cost of construction by building a single-lane deck. I cannot see any reason why we might want to disagree.[33]

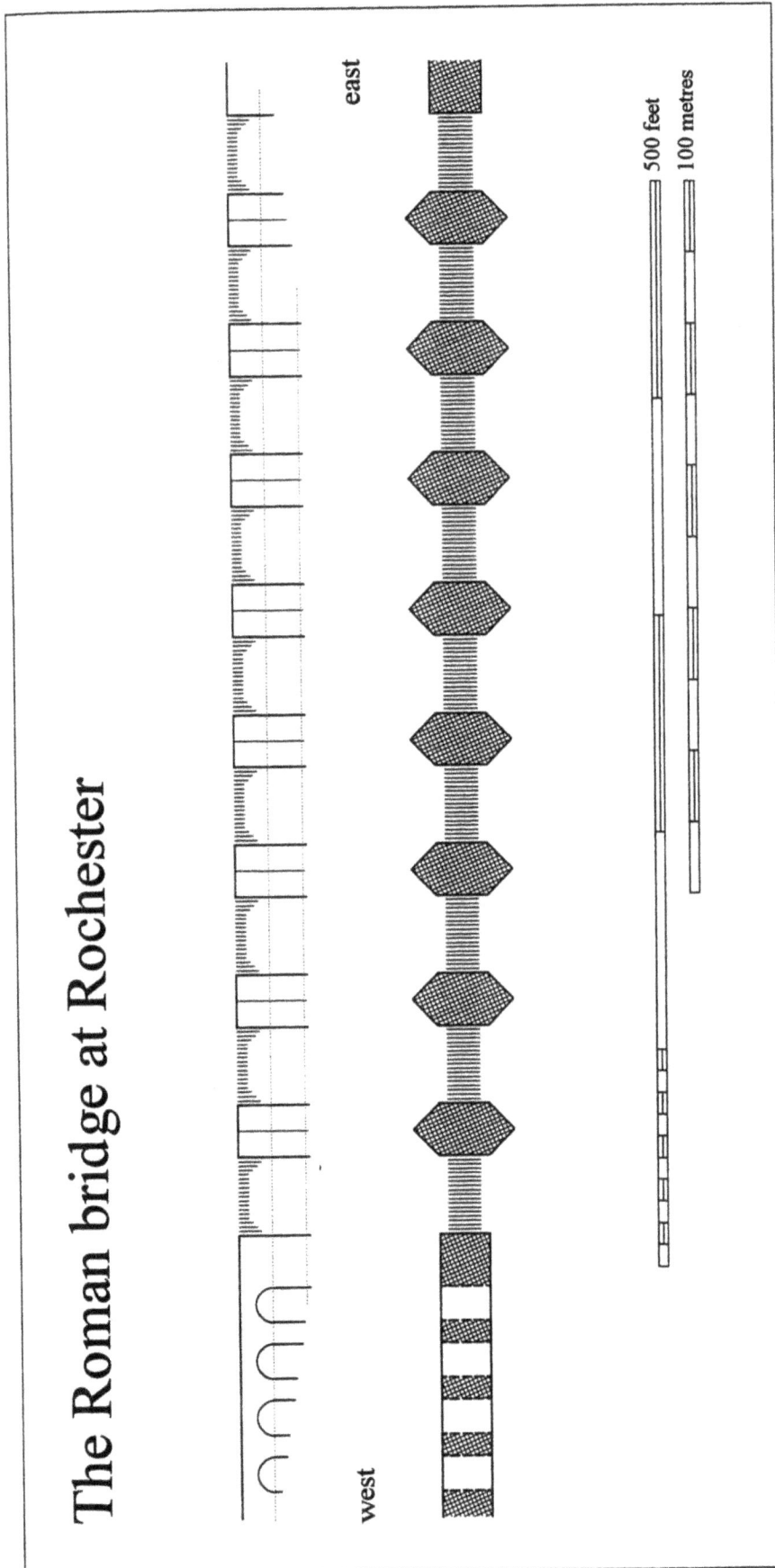

Fig. 10. A reconstruction of the Roman bridge at Rochester.

Elevation

Plan

0   Scale of feet   50

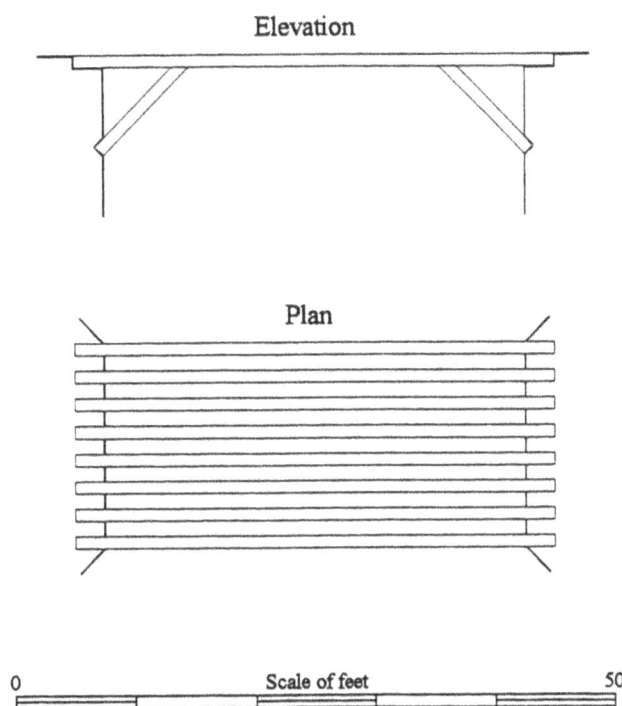

Fig. 11. The design envisaged by Essex (1785)
for the timber frames carrying the deck.

A wooden deck, exposed to the weather, subjected to wear and tear, cannot be expected to last for very long. The timber cracks and warps; here and there it starts to rot. Even if the woodwork is skilfully constructed and carefully maintained, its useful life will be measured in decades. During the last hundred years of the bridge's existence, the documentation relating to its repair survives in some quantity; and to judge from this it would always have been a rare event for twenty years to go by without some part of the timber structure demanding to be replaced.

Whenever this happened, the carpenter in charge would, in some respects, have been free to decide for himself whether to reproduce the existing design, or whether to try something new. For instance, although there must always have existed protective structures along either side of the roadway – kerbs to prevent vehicles from skidding off the edge, railings for the safety of pedestrians – their design may well have varied from time to time.[34] On the other hand, some major features of the design would have been effectively predetermined, because they were registered in the masonry. At the very least, there must have been rows of slots, along the edges of the piers, into which the ends of the beams were

fitted. Even if all the woodwork vanished, therefore, the slots would still be there, dictating the number, size, and spacing of the beams required.[35] To that extent, the design of the deck would have to stay the same, however often the timber components were replaced: it could only be altered by sending in a squad of masons to remodel the faces of the piers.

It must have crossed people's minds from time to time that much trouble and expense would be saved if the spans were rebuilt in stone. This never happened; and the basic reason (apart from all the usual excuses for doing nothing) would seem to be that medieval engineers were not prepared to risk building arches of the size required to fit the existing piers. When it was finally decided to build a stone bridge, it was also decided to build it completely new, with a larger number of (presumably smaller) openings. Very soon, the new bridge started causing trouble,[36] due, no doubt, to the settling of its foundations. If the engineer who designed the new bridge had been willing to use the old piers, that problem might perhaps have been avoided.

45

NOTES

1 James Essex (1722-1784) is a very interesting character. He has attracted attention from architectural historians because of his importance as a precursor of the Gothic Revival (Stewart 1950; Colvin 1978, pp. 297-300). He also has an important place in the history of archaeology, for his success in demonstrating that techniques of structural and stylistic analysis could lead to definite conclusions independently of written evidence – or even in the absence of written evidence.

2 Apart from Essex, the persons involved in the story are Samuel Denne (1730-1799), Thomas Fisher (d. 1786), Richard Gough (1735-1809), Owen Manning (1721-1801), and John Nichols (1745-1826). All appear in the *Dictionary of National Biography*, though Fisher only in the article about his son, also named Thomas. The letters cited here were all published in the sixth volume of Nichols's *Illustrations of the literary history of the eighteenth century*, which appeared posthumously in 1831, edited by J. B. Nichols. They are likely to have been abridged, in line with the policy stated in the editor's preface (p. v).

3 The authorship of this chapter was disclosed in a letter from one of the other contributors, William Shrubsole, published in *The Gentleman's Magazine*, lvii (1787), 1052. A batch of letters from Denne to Fisher survives (British Library, Egerton 926).

4 The author of this section is referred to by Denne, in letters to Gough and Fisher, as 'the person whom Fisher employed to write that chapter' (Nichols 1831, pp. 609-10) and 'the person employed by you to draw up the chapter of the Bridge' (Egerton 926, fol. 20). This means, I suppose, that the 'person' was paid for his work (i.e. was nobody whom Denne would have treated as an equal). Whoever he was, this author took *pera* to mean 'pier'; in fact he took it to mean a free-standing pier, so his bridge consists of ten spans (Fisher 1772, pp. 44-5). The total length of the bridge is 26½ yards, 'equal to 431 feet, which corresponds, nearly, to the present breadth of the river at that place'; the spans are equal, and each about 43 feet long. The total number of beams is 28 (by virtue of Lambarde's misprint), and that allows three beams for each span, 'excepting the two extreme arches, where two might have been sufficient'.

5 Denne to Gough, dd. Wilmington, 23 August 1783 (Nichols 1831, pp. 609-10).

6 I take this to mean, not that Denne had consulted the original manuscript, but that he had looked at Hearne's (1720) edition, where the bridgework text is reproduced at second hand from Lambarde (1596). Denne had in his possession the copy of Hearne's book which had formerly belonged to his father, John Denne, archdeacon of Rochester (Pegge 1784). That copy is now in the Parker Library, Corpus Christi College, Cambridge, as Dr Nigel Wilkins has kindly confirmed for me.

7 Manning to Gough, dd. Godalming, 18 September 1783 (Nichols 1831, p. 304, note).

8 This figure seems to have come from Fisher's *History* (above, note 4); it is certainly not right.

9 Essex to Gough, dd. Cambridge, 22 September 1783 (Nichols 1831, pp. 303-4). A rough draft and a copy of this letter survive among Essex's papers (British Library, Add. 6763, fols. 35, 34); on the evidence of this copy I have made a few small corrections to the printed text. On the same page as the draft there is a pencilled diagram, followed by some calculations relating to the length and breadth of the bridge.

10 Here Essex's arithmetic was wrong; but he put it right later.

11 Essex to Gough, dd. Cambridge, 8 November 1783 (Nichols 1831, p. 305).

12 The copy which Essex kept for himself is also to be found among his papers (Add. 6763, fols. 29-30, 32-33; fol. 31 is a fragment of a rough draft). A few scribal errors occurring in this copy apparently did not occur in the copy sent to Gough. Otherwise the printed text (Essex 1785) is practically identical with the manuscript copy, except that the spelling and punctuation have been normalized, doubtless by the printer.

13 Denne to Gough, dd. Wilmington, 16 April 1784 (Nichols 1831, pp. 610-11).

14 Essex to Gough, dd. Cambridge, 3 May 1784 (Nichols 1831, p. 309).

15 Perhaps he had misread the map in Fisher's *History*, which is drawn with north at the bottom.

16 Luard 1890, vol. 2, p. 490, from British Library, Cotton Nero D.ii, fol. 174r. Eighteenth-century antiquaries knew this chronicle from the excerpts printed in Wharton's *Anglia sacra* (1691); Essex relied on the derivative account given in Fisher's *History*.

17 On 16 November 1261 the king 'took the city into his hands', overriding the charter by which he had granted it to the citizens (above, p. 26); he did this, we are told, 'on the ground that during the troubles in the realm it was needful that the men of the city should be fully obedient to him' (*Calendar of charter rolls 1427-1516*, p. 3). On 11 July 1262 the sheriff of Kent was ordered to pay four men a sum of £25 5s 5d 'due to them for timber lately taken for the works of Rochester bridge and the town gates, and to make breastworks (*beretachias*) round the town' (*Calendar of liberate rolls 1260-7*, p. 104); the corresponding entry in the sheriff's account on the pipe roll for 1261-2 is cited by Brown and Colvin (1963, p. 809, note 7). So the fortifications on the bridge appear to have been part of a scheme to strengthen the city's defences, after the king had taken direct control of it.

18 Salzman (1967, p. 238) cites an inventory of the stores at Westminster in 1329 which includes eleven beams of 37 feet and sixteen of 50 feet. He comments that a length of 'anything much over 30 feet was unusual, especially after the middle of the fourteenth century'.

19 In other words, if the length is increased by 10 per cent, the deflection increases by more than 40 per cent; if the length is increased by 20 per cent, the deflection increases by more than 100 per cent.

20 There is a common-sense argument which leads to the same conclusion. To make the bridge as long as possible, we need to make each span as long as possible; so we cannot allow any span to be shorter than the others. Thus, by maximizing the spans, we also equalize them.

21 Just counting the three main spans, the modern bridge has a waterway of 140 + 170 + 140 = 450 feet.

22 As far back as we have any information, the tidal range at Rochester has been in the order of 15-18 feet. Though we cannot be sure, I think we have to proceed on the assumption (pending proof to the contrary) that the hydrographic régime has always been roughly the same. If so, the piers would need to be well over 30 feet high, in the deepest part of the river.

23 A description of the newly completed bridge, with an engraved view of it, can be found in *The Illustrated London News*, xxix (16 August 1856), 169. The railway bridge was apparently more or less finished by that time, though a regular passenger service did not begin till March 1858 (White 1961, p. 40).

24 Repairs to the drawbridge were accounted for by Sir Simon de Burgh in 1375-6 (E 101/480/4) and by Sir John de Newenton in 1379-80, 1385-8, and 1389-90 (attested only by the summary entries appearing on the foreign account rolls: *Lists and indexes*, vol. 11, p. 119). By the time of these last repairs the construction of the new bridge was already well under way (above, p. 32). A few years later, after the new bridge had been completed, the king made himself responsible for providing it with a drawbridge like the one on the old bridge. This task was assigned to the clerk of the king's works in 1395, and seems to have been finished by 1398-9 (Brown and Colvin 1963, pp. 814-5).

25 Probably by Walter de Merton, formerly the king's chancellor, who as bishop of Rochester (1274-1277) was patron of Strood hospital.

26 The dating implied is after 1199, when Johan came to the throne, but before 1214, when Gilbert died. Since Gilbert was out of the country from 1209 onwards, returning only one year before he died, it is probably safe to sharpen up the date to 1199×1209. I am not aware of any contemporary evidence relating to this transaction. The inquiry held in 1276 reports that the bishop asked the king to make a contribution towards the cost of repairing the 'bridge' (i.e. the approach to the bridge), 'and the king ordered the sheriff of Kent to pay him 40s. for that purpose'. A note of this payment ought to appear in the pipe rolls (the fact was mentioned, I suppose, precisely because it was thought to be easily verifiable), but I have not been able to find it.

27 In the diagram (Fig. 8) I show the bishop's wharf on the upstream side, on the assumption that this was the same structure which later became the approach to the new bridge.

28 The chapel is mentioned only incidentally: we know that it existed in 1277, but we cannot be sure that it was part of bishop Gilbert's original plan. I would guess that it was.

29 In fourteenth-century English the word *brigge* could mean a jetty, a bridge-like structure projecting into a river but not extending the whole way across it. There was a jetty in London, for example, called *Tempelbrigge* (Riley 1868, pp. 306, 376). At Rochester, in 1339-40, the contractors operating the ferry put themselves to the expense of building 'two wooden bridges' (*ii pont' lign'*, E 101/507/20): presumably these were jetties, one on either side of the river.

30 In Fig. 10 I have assumed that the viaduct consisted of four 16-foot arches carried by 10-foot piers. The approach to the bridge is required to look like a bridge – enough so for people to think of calling it a 'bridge' – but the rest is all gratuitous.

As regards the shape of this viaduct, we have no means of deciding whether one guess is better or worse than another.

31 The struts are an indispensable feature of the design: the frame would not be adequately strong without them (Appendix 3). Though Essex does not say so, it seems to me that any competent carpenter, asked to build such a frame, would want to incorporate some transverse bracing too.

32 A glance at the second volume of Hasted's *History* would have saved him from falling into this trap. Hasted understood perfectly well that the text was referring to ploughlands (1782, p. 16, notes c and p).

33 In case the reader should think of asking this question, the answer is that three beams would barely be enough, even for a single-lane bridge. With just three beams, the failure of one beam is more or less sure to have catastrophic consequences. It is obviously more sensible to spread the load across a larger number of (slightly smaller) beams.

34 We have only to imagine what it would be like crossing the bridge on a wet and windy day to realize that railings would be indispensable. The fact that there is no mention of them in the bridgework text cannot be taken to mean that they did not exist: it was not the author's remit to tell us everything. He does not tell us, for instance, that to build the bridge we shall need a supply of nails – but obviously we have to have some means of fixing the planks to the beams.

35 These hypothetical slots provide one possible explanation for the implicit distinction made by the bridgework text between the actual number of beams to be laid – three per span – and the total number of beams (above, p. 24). Suppose there were seven slots existing in the masonry: the text would then be saying that four slots should be ignored.

36 Major repairs due to structural failure were carried out in 1409-10 (when one of the piers began to give way), in 1423-6 (when two of the arches started cracking), and in 1445 (when one arch collapsed). All this information comes from the Bridge Wardens' annual account rolls (Becker 1930, pp. 83-9; Britnell 1994, pp. 70-3). The accounts cease after 1479, but the bridge did not cease causing trouble. On the contrary, a little later it had to be more or less completely rebuilt (Britnell 1994, pp. 73-5).

6

Conclusion

Though I have refrained from saying so till now, I think we can take it for granted that the bridge in question – the bridge which existed in the twelfth century, and which continued to exist till the end of the fourteenth century – was a specimen of Roman engineering.[1]

There is some evidence suggesting that it was built in the fourth century. On the left bank, Strood High Street perpetuates the line of the road approaching the bridge. In 1897, when a storm-water drain was laid down along this line, George Payne kept an eye on the work (Payne 1898, pp. 4-7). The excavations were deep enough to reach the alluvial mud (roughly 8½ feet below the level of the modern street) across which the Roman engineers had had to construct their road. Driven into this mud, Payne found, were 'numerous oak piles about 4 feet in length, with pieces of wood laid at intervals across them'; and on top of this wooden substructure was a layer of flints and rubble, 3½ feet thick, forming a raised foundation for the road.[2] Reportedly from this layer of rubble came five Roman coins, the latest of which was a coin struck between 293 and 305.[3] If it can be taken at face value (of which I am very doubtful), this evidence proves that the approach road on the Strood side was not built before the turn of the fourth century; and with further reservations the same might be thought to apply to the bridge itself.

A fourth-century bridge, of course, could not be the earliest Roman bridge at Rochester. On the right bank, the line of the road approaching the bridge, approximately preserved by Rochester High Street (Fig. 1), does not coincide with the alignment of the bridge: as was noticed by Wheeler (1932, p. 85), the road appears to be aiming at a point some distance downstream, as if that is where it expects the bridge to be. So perhaps we need to think in terms of two successive bridges. The earlier bridge, presumably built in the first century, would have stood on the site indicated by the alignment of Rochester High Street; at some later date, possibly in the fourth century, this would have been superseded by a new bridge, built alongside it, on the upstream side.

On the Strood side, the building of this new bridge would have entailed the construction of a new approach road across the floodplain – the road discovered by Payne. On the Rochester side, a short stretch of new road would also have been required, to connect the bridge with the line of the existing road. More than that, if the bridge dates from the fourth century, it postdates the town-wall;[4] and hence, at the least, a new gate would have had to be inserted. The line of the wall at this point is slightly uncertain, and nothing is known about the gate (or gates) facing towards the river. But there is some evidence which seems to show that in fact this whole stretch of wall – between the bridge and the north-west angle – was differently constructed from the rest (Harrison and Flight 1969, pp. 76-7). In particular, Payne reports seeing part of this wall exposed in 1889: the mortar was pink, and the masonry included a double course of tiles (Payne 1895, p. 8). The Roman town-wall was not traced out completely until a few years later, in 1892-3;[5] but it then became clear that everywhere else the wall was built with buff-coloured mortar, without any use of tiles. So the wall along the riverfront appears to have been totally rebuilt, perhaps on a new alignment, in a style resembling (for example) the late third-century work at Richborough.

This it begins to seem possible that all these alterations – a new stretch of town wall, a new gate, a new bridge, a new approach road on the left bank – were elements in a single scheme, carried out in some coordinated manner. Moreover, this Rochester scheme could be seen as part of a larger project, the fortification of the Saxon shore. I do not disguise the fact that the evidence for all of this is very thin; but perhaps there may be an opportunity, sooner or later, to clarify some of these matters through excavation.

NOTES

1 This question was rather weakly discussed by Arnold (1921) and Robson (1921). Some brief but sensible comments can be found in Wheeler (1932, p. 85).

48

2 The paved surface of the road, thought by Payne to be Roman, is fairly sure to be of much later date — subsequent to the construction of the new bridge at the end of the fourteenth century (Thornhill 1979).

3 The coins are an odd assortment: one of Nerva (96-98), two of Antoninus Pius (138-161), one of Gordianus III (238-244), and one of Galerius Maximianus as Caesar (293-305). I assume that the workmen were rewarded for finding coins, and the danger which follows from that is obvious enough.

4 The wall appears to have been built in the early third century (Harrison and Williams 1980, p. 21).

5 *Archaeologia Cantiana*, xx (1893), p. xlvii.

Appendices

Appendix 1
The bridgework text

Those readers who (like me) do not have easy access to the facsimile edition may find the following transcription of some use. The text is given line for line as it appears in the manuscript (*Privilegia*, fols. 164v-165v, 166v-167r). I have expanded all the abbreviations (except for numerals) and added some punctuation where consistency seems to demand it; but I have not emended the wording in any way.

In the rewritten portion of the Latin version (fol. 164v) the words *et de ufenhylle* have been added in the margin, near the bottom of the page, by a still later hand (above, p. 7, note 16). They are marked for insertion after *aclea* in line 23.

Copies of the Latin version are included in two later compilations from Rochester. In Brooks's notation, the manuscripts in question are C = *Custumale Roffense* (Strood, Rochester upon Medway Studies Centre, DRc/R2), fols. 63v-64v (mid thirteenth century), and D = *Registrum temporalium* (Maidstone, Centre for Kentish Studies, DRb/Ar2), fols. 140v-141r (early fourteenth century). C and D are both free in their treatment of place-names but otherwise fairly accurate, so the textual relationships are difficult to work out. The passage erased from B = *Privilegia* is missing from both: they close up the gap between Eccles and Horsted without any sign that something has been omitted; there are also two shared errors (for example, in paragraph 9, *tres suliuas* B, *sulliuas* CD, with the numeral omitted). At the same time, there are some places where D agrees with B against C (for example, in paragraphs 5-6, *summittere ... supponere* BD, *supponere ... summittere* C). From these few clues, it seems fairly clear that D was not copied from C, and that neither D nor C was copied directly from B.

164v (later hand)
**Hęc descriptio demonstrat aperte unde
debeat pons de rouecestra restaurari, quotiens
P R I M V M eiusdem   fuerit fractus.**
ciuitatis episcopus incipit operari in orientali brachio primam peram de terra, deinde tres uirgatas plancas ponere, et
tres suliuas, id est tres magnas trabes
supponere. Et hoc faciet de borcstealla,
et de cuclestana, et de freondesberia, et de sto-
che. Postea secunda pera pertinet ad gillinge-
ham, et de cætham, et unam uirgatam plancas
ponere, et .iii. suliuas supponere. Deinde tercia pera pertinet iterum ad episcopum ciuitatis eiusdem, et duas uirgatas et dimidiam plancas ponere, et .iiiᵉᵉ. suliuas supponere, et
hoc fiet de hallingis, et de trotescliua, et
de meallingis, et de fleotes, et de stanes,

et de pinindene, et de falceham. Postea quarta
pera pertinet ad regem, et .iiiᵉᵉ. et dimidiam
uirgatam plancas ponere, et .iiiᵉᵉ. suliuas
supponere, et hoc debet fieri de æilesforda,
et de toto illo lesto quod ad illud manerium
pertinet, et de supermontaneis, et de aclea, et de
smalalande, et de cusintunæ, et de dudeslande, et

165r (main hand)
de gisleardes lande, et de wldeham, et de
burhham, et de aclesse, : : : : : : :
: : : : : : : : : : : : : : : : : :
: , et de horsteda, et de fearnlega, et
de terstane, et de cealca, et de hænhersta,
et de hathdune. Deinde quinta pera est
archiepiscopi, .iiiiᵒʳ. uirgatas plancas ponere,
et tres suliuas summittere, et hoc debet
fieri de wroteham, et de mæidesstana,
et de oteringaberiga, et de netlasteda,
et de duobus peccham, et de hæselholte, et
de mæreuuurtha, et de lilleburna, et de
suuanatuna, et de offeham, et de dictune,
et de westerham. Postea sexta pera debet fieri de holingeburna, et de toto
illo lesto quę ad hoc pertinet, .iiiiᵒʳ. uirgatas plancas ponere, et tres suliuas supponere. Septimam et octauam peram debent facere homines de hou, et quattuor
et dimidiam uirgatas plancas ponere, et
sex suliuas supponere. Deinde nona
pera quę ultima est in occidentali brachio est iterum archiepiscopi, .iiiiᵒʳ. uirgatas
plancas ponere, et tres suliuas summit-

165v)
tere, et hęc debet fieri de northfleta, et
de cliua, et de heahham, et de denituna,
et de meletuna, et de hludesduna, et
de meapeham, et de snodilanda, et de ber-
lingæs, et de ` pe´dlesuurthe, et de omnibus il-
lis hominibus qui manent in illa ualle.
Et sciendum est quod omnes illę suliuę quę
in ponte illo ponentur tantę grossitudi-
nis debent esse, ut bene possint sustine-
re omnia grauia pondera superiacentium
plancarum, et omnium desuper pertranseun-
tium rerum.

166v (later hand)
Þis is þære bricce geweorc on hrouecæstre.
Her syndon genamad þa land þe man hi of
scæl weorcan. Ærest þære burge biscop fehð
on þone earm to wercene þa land peran, and þreo
gyrda to þillianæ, and .iii. sylla to lyccan-
ne, þæt is of borcstealle, and of cucclestane, and
of frinondesbyrig, and of stoce. Þanne seo oðer per gebyraþ to gyllingeham, and to
cætham, and an gyrd to þillanne, and .iii. sylla
to leccanne. Þonne seo þridde per gebyrað eft þam biscope, and þridde healf
gyrd to þillianne, and .iii. sylla to leccanne, of
heallingan, and of trotescliue, and of meallingan,
and of fliote, and of stane, and of pinindene, and of
falchenham. Þonne : : is se feorðe þe per þæs
cinges, and fiorðe healf gyrd to þillanne, and sylla
.iii. to leccanne, of æglesforda, and of ellan þam

51

læþe þe þær to liþ, and of ufanhylle, and of aclea,
and of þam smalanlande, and of cusintune, and of dudeslande, and of gisleardeslande, and of wuldeham,
and of burhham, and of æcclesse,
                          , and of horstede, and of fearn
lege, and of tærstane, and of cealce, and of hennhyste, and
of ædune. Þonne is sy fifte per þæs arcebiscope,
                                                    to

167r (main hand)
wroteham, and to mægþanstane, and to woþringa-
byran, and to netlestede, and to þam twam peccham, and to hæselholte, and to mæranwyrþe, and
to lillanburnan, and to swanatune, and to offaham,
and to dictune, and to westerham, and .iiii. gyrda to
þyllanne, and .iii. selle to leccanne. Þonne is syo
syoxte per to holinganburnan, and to eallan
þam læþe, and .iiii. gyrda to þelliene, and .iii. sylla
to leccenne. Þonne is syo syoueþe and syo eah-
teþe per to howaran lande to wyrcenne, and
fifte healf gyrd to þillanne, and .vi. sylla to lyc-
canne. Þonne is syo nigaþa per þæs arcebi-
scopes, þæt is syo land per æt þam west ænde,
to flyote, and to his cliue, and to hehham, and to dene-
tune, and to melantune, and to hludesdune, and to
meapeham, and to snodilande, and to berlingan,
and to peadleswyrþe, and ealla þa dænewaru, and .iiii.
gyrdu to þilianne, and þryo sylle to leccanne.

Appendix 2
Commissions of inquiry

From time to time, commissioners were appointed by the king, with instructions to ascertain which places were responsible for repairing the bridge at Rochester. During the fourteenth century this happened every few years; the relevant entries on the patent rolls are conveniently cited by Brooks (1994, p. 38, note 94). Presumably on most occasions the commissioners obeyed their orders and summarized their findings in a written report, but only six such reports are known to have survived. For reference I list them here.

(1) A report, circa 1230, covering the whole bridge but referring specially to spans 4 and 6. Surviving only in a version which includes an interpolation made at Christ Church relating to the manor of Hollingbourne. Printed in full by Lambarde (1576, pp. 304-6), from his own copy of a copy by Nicholas Wotton, derived from one of the Canterbury registers; printed again by Brooks (1994, pp. 367-9). For the dating, see p. 8, note 24.

(2-3) A pair of reports, dated 28 May 1276 and 22 May 1277 respectively, relating to the western bridgehead. The originals survive. Not available in print, but summarized in *Calendar of inquisitions miscellaneous (Chancery)*, vol. 1, p. 315 (no. 1026), p. 323 (no. 1061).

(4) A report dated 1 March 1340, referring to span 5 alone. Surviving as a copy on the Coram Rege roll for the Easter term 1340. Printed in full by Flower (1915, pp. 204-8).

(5) A report dated 29 June 1343, covering the whole bridge but referring specially to spans 1 and 3. The original survives (C 145/149/24). Not available in print, but summarized in *Calendar of inquisitions miscellaneous (Chancery)*, vol. 2, pp. 459-60 (no. 1846).

(6) A report dated 12 June 1355, covering the whole bridge. The original seems to have been lost. It is not listed where one would expect to find it, in *Calendar of inquisitions miscellaneous (Chancery)*, vol. 3, pp. 69-77; and John Cassidy of the Public Record Office, who has kindly made a search for the document at my request, has not been able to trace it. A transcript survives among the Thorpe papers (Society of Antiquaries 198/1, part II, fol. 151): I am grateful to Bernard Nurse for discovering this copy, and for having it microfilmed for me. Another transcript is to be found in Sir Roger Manwood's 'A true discourse of the auncyent wodden and present stoned bridge at Rochester', compiled in 1586 (cf. Gibson 1994, p. 114, note 27): I owe this reference to Dr James M. Gibson. Much of the text is in close agreement with that of the previous report (no. 5); whoever wrote this new report seems to have had a copy of that one in front of him. (On the other hand, there is nothing to suggest that he had a copy of the bridgework text in its unedited form.)

By permission of the Society of Antiquaries of London, I print the text of this report as it was transcribed for Thorpe; I have divided it into paragraphs and added some punctuation but otherwise made no changes.

Inquisitio capta coram Galfrido de Saye et sociis suis justiciariis domini regis, virtute commissionis domini regis sibi directe super defectibus pontis Roffensis, die Veneris proxima post festum sancti Barnabe apostoli, anno regis Edwardi tertii a conquestu vicesimo nono, per sacramentum Rogeri atte Hethe, Bartholomei at Grove, Johannis Lovekyn, Thome Barnes, Johannis Kettle, Johannis Ram, Willelmi Woodyere, Thome Philpott, Johannis Gurdon, Johannis Athall, Richardi de Shamell, Johannis Ferrour &c.

Qui dicunt quod est quedam placea longitudinis triginta pedum adjacens wharfe orientali, quam homines de Frendsburye ex parte boreali debent facere et civitas Roffen' ex parte australi, que quidem placea quondam fuit Johannis Englishe et nunc est Johannis de Cosington, et dicta placea tempore dicti Johannis Englishe bene et sufficienter edificata et warvata fuit contra defensionem aque de Medewaye, et nunc adnichilata est per fluxum et refluxum aque predicte, et sic nunc vastata, quod licet pons Roffen' et warva predicta bene et sufficienter reparati fuissent vix aliqui transeuntes cum equis aut carectis sine periculo evadere possunt; que quidem placea non potest reparari minus quam tresdecim libris sex solidis et octo denariis.

Item dicunt quod villate de Borestall, Cocklestane, Frendsburye et Stoke, tenentes episcopi Roffensis, debent incipere facere warvam predictam in orientali brachio versus civitatem Roffensem tam opus ligneum quam terreum usque ad secundam peram, et sic vocatur prima pera; que quidem non minus possunt quam nonaginta tribus libris sex solidis et octo denariis ad presens reparari.

Dicunt etiam quod villate de Chettham et Gillingham facere debent secundam peram; que quidem pera non minus potest reparari ad presens quam quinque libris.

Dicunt etiam quod villate de Halling, Trotescleyffe, Malling, Southflete, Stone, Penynden et Faukeham facere debent tertiam peram; que quidem pera non minus potest reparari quam decem libris.

Dicunt etiam quod villate de Eyllesford, Ickles, Ovenhill, Smaleborne, Cosington, Doddeslonde, Gilberdeslonde, Woldham, Burham, Horsted, Farleighe, Terston, Chalke, Henherst et Ocle facere debent quartam peram; que quidem pera non minus potest reparari quam centum et viginti libris.

Dicunt etiam quod Wrotham, Maidestone, Wateringbery, Nettlested, East Peckham, Haselholte, Mereworth, Leyborne, Swanscombe [sic], Offham, Dycton et Westram facere debent quintam peram; que quidem non minus potest reparari quam octoginta libris.

Dicunt etiam quod Hollingborne et Eyhorne facere debent sextam peram; que quidem non minus reparari potest quam sexaginta libris.

Dicunt etiam quod homines de Hooe facere debent septimam et octavam peram; que quidem non minus possunt reparari quam sexaginta sex libris tresdecim solidis et quatuor denariis.

Dicunt etiam quod Northflete, Clyve, Higham, Denton, Milton, Loddesdone, Meapham, Snodland, Birling et Padlesworthe facere debent nonam peram; que quidem non minus potest reparari quam viginti sex libris.

Dicunt etiam quod dominus rex faciet Barbican a ponte tractivo; et non minus potest reparari quam &c [sic].

Dicunt etiam quod magistri et fratres hospitalis beate Marie de Strode facient pontem cum warva a ponte predicto tractivo usque Strode, videlicet usque ad finem eiusdem pontis ex parte occidentali; que quidem non minus potest reparari quam sexaginta libris ad presens.

Appendix 3
Strength of materials

The following remarks are all derived from elementary textbooks of engineering, and from an assortment of nineteenth-century encyclopaedias (which are generally more informative than modern ones). Though I claim no competence whatever in this field, it seems necessary to take account of engineering considerations if we want to be able to judge between alternative reconstructions of the bridge.

Rupture. Suppose that we want to know whether a loaded beam can be trusted not to break. Granted certain assumptions (viz. that the beam is simply supported and uniformly loaded), the relevant variables are the ones which enter into the following equation:

$$3ql^2 = 4Rbh^2,$$

where q is the load per unit of length (measured in pounds per inch), l, b, and h are respectively the length, breadth, and height of the beam (all measured in inches), and R is a quantity called the modulus of rupture (pounds per square inch) which represents the breaking strength of the material forming the beam.

If we know or can estimate four of these values, the formula allows us to calculate the fifth. For example, if we want to know what unit load can safely be supported by a beam of given material and given dimensions, we rearrange the formula in this way:

$$q = \frac{4Rbh^2}{3l^2};$$

if instead we want to know how long the beam can be, we set

$$l^2 = \frac{4Rbh^2}{3q};$$

and take the square root (not forgetting to divide the answer by 12 if we want the length in feet).

If we plan to use beams of oak, a suitable estimate for R is 7632 lb in^{-2}. This figure is in accordance with the guidelines adopted by the Royal Engineers in the nineteenth century;[1] the actual value, of course, will vary greatly between one piece of oak and another. With regard to the load, the Royal Engineers made it their rule that a bridge ought to be capable of carrying 240 pounds per square foot, which is $1^2/_3$ lb in^{-2}. To calculate the unit load, we have to consider the specifications of some proposed design. In the deck designed by Essex, for example, the beams are 12 inches square and 15 inches apart; so each beam supports a strip of roadway 27 inches broad.[2] Hence, for each inch of its length, the load carried by the beam is $27 \times 1^2/_3 = 45$ lb. Now if we ask how long the span can be, the answer we get (assuming the beam to be simply supported) is

$$l^2 = \frac{4 \times 7632 \times 12 \times 12^2}{3 \times 45},$$

so that l works out to be roughly 52 feet.

This calculation neglects the weight of the deck itself, which increases the load significantly. If we take it that oak weighs 60 lb ft^{-3}, and if we assume that the planking is 4 inches thick, the additional load will be roughly 9 lb for each inch of length. Repeating the calculation with $q = 54$, the answer we get is a little less than 48 feet.

The equation given above does not incorporate any factor of safety.[3] Needless to say, wooden beams tend to have all sorts of hidden weaknesses, invisible even to an expert eye. For this and other reasons, the Royal Engineers, working with timber, insisted on multiplying by a factor of 4 at least, and felt more comfortable with 6. (Modern engineers would prefer a still larger figure, say 10.) If we wanted to achieve a safety factor of 4, without increasing the number or size of the beams, we should have to reduce the length of the span by half. In other words, with Essex's design, we cannot safely allow the spans to have an unsupported length exceeding 24 feet (which is why Essex assumed that struts would be indispensable).

Elasticity. An alternative way of approaching the problem is to ask by how much the beam is likely to bend. The arithmetic involved here is more complicated, but not horrifically so. For anyone owning a computer, or a programmable calculator, it ought to be easy enough. Under the same assumptions as before, the curve into which the beam deflects (provided it does not bend so far that it actually starts to break) is described by this equation:

$$y = \frac{qx}{2Ebh^3}(l^3 - 2lx^2 + x^3),$$

where y is the deflection (measured downwards) and x is the horizontal distance (measured from one of the supports). The new term E is a quantity called the modulus of elasticity, which expresses the stiffness of the material. For oak, the appropriate value is in the neighbourhood of 1½ million pounds per square inch; the value which I have chosen to work with is $1 \cdot 456 \times 10^6$ lb in^{-2}, 650 tons per square inch.

To find the maximum deflection, occurring at the centre of the span, we set $x = \frac{1}{2}l$. The equation then simplifies to this:

$$y_{max} = \frac{5ql^4}{32Ebh^3}.$$

If we opt to specify a value for the maximum deflection that we are willing to tolerate, we can rearrange the equation so that it gives us a value for the maximum length of span. Assuming we want to ensure that the deflection expressed as a fraction of the length does not exceed 1/200 (which is what the more generous manuals recommend), we set

$$l^3 = \frac{32Ebh^3}{1000q}.$$

For Essex's design, minus the struts, with $q = 54$, the maximum length works out to be slightly less than 22 feet. This agrees quite closely with the result we arrived at before, through calculations based on the breaking strength.

In the case of a beam supported by struts – as for any beam which is not supported only at the ends – the deflection curve takes on a more sinuous shape. I have made various calculations, for the planks and struts (which also bend) as well as for the beams, but do not propose to explain them in detail here. In the end, after all the arithmetic, the conclusion is a simple one. For a frame with the proportions envisaged by Essex (roughly 1:3:1),

the struts make a world of difference. With the struts in place, no part of the frame will bend by more than 1 inch. Without the struts, the deck would sag by 9 inches in the middle – if it did not start to give way (the safety factor being less than 2). Given these proportions, very nearly the whole of the load is carried by the struts, almost none of it by the tops of the piers. In fact, if the struts were any shorter than this, the ends of the beams would have to be held down, or else they would tend to hoist themselves out of their sockets. To put it simply, the piers serve to support the struts, and the struts support the deck.

Under these conditions, the soundness of the structure is going to depend on the quality of the workmanship, much more than on the properties of the material. With adequate bracing, the movements which result from the elasticity of the timber will be negligibly small. What matters is the accuracy with which the components are cut to shape and fitted together. If the carpenters do a good job, the deck will be firm and long-lasting; if they do not, it will soon begin to shake itself apart.

NOTES

1 The guidelines were based on a long series of experiments performed by attaching weights to miniature beams 12 inches long and 1 inch square. With oak, the conclusion was that a beam of this size could be trusted not to break as long as the weight did not exceed 424 lb. Taking $R = (3Pl)/(2bh^2)$, the formula which applies in the case of a load P concentrated at the centre of the beam, we get $R = 7632$ lb in^{-2}.

2 Strictly speaking, the load is not evenly distributed among the beams; but the variation is negligible provided that the number of beams is fairly large. (With three beams, however, the central beam would carry more than half the load, the outer beams each less than a quarter.)

3 Without knowing the details behind them, I cannot make much sense of the calculations reported by Brooks (1994, p. 25); but I suspect that by 'absolute limits' is meant 'the limits which would apply if one dispensed with a factor of safety'.

Bibliography

A. A. Arnold, 'The earliest Rochester bridge: was it built by the Romans?', *Archaeologia Cantiana*, xxxv (1921), 127-38.

M. J. Becker, *Rochester Bridge – 1387-1856 – a history of its early years compiled from the Wardens' accounts* (London, 1930).

W. de Gray Birch (ed.), *Cartularium saxonicum*, 3 vols. (London, 1885-93).

R. H. Britnell, 'Rochester Bridge, 1381-1530', in N. Yates and J. M. Gibson (eds.), *Traffic and politics: the construction and management of Rochester Bridge, AD 43-1993* (Woodbridge, 1994), 41-106.

N. P. Brooks, *The early history of the church of Canterbury* (Leicester, 1984).

N. P. Brooks, 'Church, crown and community: public work and seigneurial responsibilities at Rochester bridge', in T. Reuter (ed.), *Warriors and churchmen in the high Middle Ages: essays presented to Karl Leyser* (London and Rio Grande, Ohio, 1992), 1-20.

N. P. Brooks, 'Rochester Bridge, AD 43-1381', in N. Yates and J. M. Gibson (eds.), *Traffic and politics: the construction and management of Rochester Bridge, AD 43-1993* (Woodbridge, 1994), 1-40 (with Appendix C, pp. 362-9).

R. A. Brown and H. M. Colvin, 'The royal castles 1066-1485', in R. A. Brown, H. M. Colvin and A. J. Taylor (eds.), *The history of the king's works*, ii (HMSO, 1963), 553-894.

J. Burtt, 'On the archives of Rochester', *Archaeologia Cantiana*, vi (1866), 108-19.

A. Campbell (ed.), *Charters of Rochester* (Anglo-Saxon Charters I, 1973).

H. M. Colvin, *A biographical dictionary of British architects 1660-1840* (London, 1978).

D. C. Douglas (ed.), *The Domesday Monachorum of Christ Church Canterbury* (London, 1944).

J. Essex, 'A description and plan of the ancient timber bridge at Rochester', *Archaeologia*, vii (1785), 395-400.

T. Fisher (comp.), *The history and antiquities of Rochester and its environs* (Rochester, 1772).

C. Flight, 'Four vernacular texts from the pre-conquest archive of Rochester cathedral', *Archaeologia Cantiana*, cxv (1996 for 1995), 121-53.

C. Flight and A. C. Harrison, 'The southern defences of medieval Rochester', *Archaeologia Cantiana*, ciii (1987 for 1986), 1-26.

C. T. Flower, *Public works in mediaeval law*, 2 vols. (Selden Society, 1915-23).

J. M. Gibson, 'Rochester Bridge, 1530-1660', in N. Yates and J. M. Gibson (eds.), *Traffic and politics: the construction and management of Rochester Bridge, AD 43-1993* (Woodbridge, 1994), 107-59.

A. Gray, *The London, Chatham & Dover Railway* (Rainham, 1984).

A. Gray, *South Eastern Railway* (Midhurst, 1990).

J. Harris, *The history of Kent*, vol. 1 (London, 1719).

A. C. Harrison and C. Flight, 'The Roman and medieval defences of Rochester in the light of recent excavations', *Archaeologia Cantiana*, lxxxiii (1969 for 1968), 55-104.

A. C. Harrison and D. Williams, 'Excavation at Prior's Gate House, Rochester 1976-77', *Archaeologia Cantiana*, xcv (1980 for 1979), 19-36.

Harvester Press, *Church authority and power in medieval and early modern Britain – the episcopal registers – part 8 – registers of the bishops of Chichester (1396-1675), Gloucester (1541-1681), and Rochester (1319-1683)* (Brighton, 1987).

E. Hasted, *The history and topographical survey of the county of Kent*, vol. 2 (Canterbury, 1782).

E. Hasted, *The history and topographical survey of the county of Kent*, ed. 2, 12 vols. (Canterbury, 1797-1801).

F. S. Haydon (ed.), *Eulogium historiarum sive temporis*, 3 vols. (Rolls Series IX, 1858-63).

T. Hearne (ed.), *Textus Roffensis* (Oxford, 1720).

L. C. Hector and B. F. Harvey (eds.), *The Westminster chronicle 1381-1394* (Oxford, 1982).

S. J. Herrtage (ed.), *The English Charlemagne romances – part I – Sir Ferumbras* (Early English Text Society, Extra Series XXXIV, 1879).

W. Holtzmann (ed.), *Papsturkunden in England*, vol. 2 (Berlin, 1935-6).

J. Hughes, 'On the pneumatic method adopted in constructing the foundations of the new bridge across the Medway, at Rochester', *Minutes of proceedings of the Institution of Civil Engineers,* x (1851), 353-65.

W. Illingworth and J. Caley (eds.), *Placita de Quo waranto* (Record Commission, 1818).

B. R. Kemp (ed.), *Reading Abbey cartularies*, vol. 1 (Camden Fourth Series XXXI, 1986).

N. R. Ker, *Catalogue of manuscripts containing Anglo-Saxon* (Oxford, 1957).

W. Lambard[e], *A perambulation of Kent* (London, 1576).

W. Lambarde, *A perambulation of Kent*, ed. 2 (London, 1596).

H. R. Luard (ed.), *Flores historiarum*, 3 vols. (Rolls Series XCV, London, 1890).

J. A. H. Murray (ed.), *A new English dictionary on historical principles*, vol. 7, part 2 (Oxford, 1909).

J. Nichols (ed.), *Illustrations of the literary history of the eighteenth century*, vol. 6, ed. J. B. Nichols (London, 1831).

D. Ormrod, 'Rochester Bridge, 1660-1825', in N. Yates and J. M. Gibson (eds.), *Traffic and politics: the construction and management of Rochester Bridge, AD 43-1993* (Woodbridge, 1994), 161-219.

G. Payne, 'Roman Rochester', *Archaeologia Cantiana*, xxi (1895), 1-16.

G. Payne, 'Roman discoveries', *Archaeologia Cantiana*, xxiii (1898), 1-23.

S. Pegge, 'An historical account of that venerable monument of antiquity the Textus Roffensis', in J. Nichols (ed.), *Bibliotheca topographica britannica*, no. 25 (1784), 1-32.

D. A. E. Pelteret, 'Two Old English lists of serfs', *Mediaeval Studies*, xlviii (1986), 470-513.

Pipe roll 31 Henry I, ed. J. Hunter (London, 1833, reprinted 1929).

Pipe rolls 3-4 Richard I, ed. D. M. Stenton (Pipe Roll Society, 1926).

H. T. Riley (ed.), *Memorials of London and London life* (London, 1868).

A. J. Robertson (ed.), *Anglo-Saxon charters* (Cambridge, 1939).

A. J. Robertson (ed.), *Anglo-Saxon charters*, ed. 2 (Cambridge, 1956).

C. Robinson (ed.), *The Memoranda roll of the King's Remembrancer for Michaelmas 1230 – Trinity 1231* (Pipe Roll Society, 1933).

J. J. Robson, 'Rochester bridge: the Roman bridge in masonry', *Archaeologia Cantiana*, xxxv (1921), 139-44.

Rotuli parliamentorum, 6 vols. (London, 1767-77).

W. B. Rye, 'The ancient episcopal palace at Rochester, and Bishop Fisher', *Archaeologia Cantiana*, xvii (1887), 66-76.

L. F. Salzman, *Building in England down to 1540* (Oxford, 1952, reprinted 1967).

P. H. Sawyer (ed.), *Textus Roffensis – Rochester Cathedral Library manuscript A.3.5*, 2 vols. (Early English Manuscripts in Facsimile VII and XI, Copenhagen, 1957-62).

P. H. Sawyer, *Anglo-Saxon charters: an annotated list and bibliography* (London, 1968).

E. S. Scroggs, 'The records of Rochester Bridge and of the New College of Cobham', *Archives*, ii (1954), 183-91.

S. Smiles, *Lives of the engineers*, rev. ed., 5 vols. (London, 1874-9).

D. R. Stewart, 'James Essex', *Architectural Review*, cviii (1950), 317-21.

P. Thornhill, 'Second thoughts on Strood's causeway', *Archaeologia Cantiana*, xciv (1979 for 1978), 249-55.

[J. Thorpe], *A list of the lands contributory to Rochester-bridge* (n.p., 1731).

J. Thorpe, *Registrum Roffense* (London, 1769).

J. Thorpe, *Custumale Roffense* (London, 1788).

J. K. Wallenberg, *Kentish place-names* (Uppsala, 1931).

J. K. Wallenberg, *The place-names of Kent* (Uppsala, 1934).

G. Ward, 'The list of Saxon churches in the Textus Roffensis', *Archaeologia Cantiana*, xliv (1932), 39-59.

G. Ward, 'The lathe of Aylesford in 975', *Archaeologia Cantiana*, xlvi (1934), 7-26.

H. Wharton, *Anglia sacra*, 2 vols. (London, 1691).

R. E. M. Wheeler, 'The towns of Roman Kent', in W. Page (ed.), *The Victoria County History of the county of Kent*, iii (London, 1932), 60-101.

H. P. White, *A regional history of the railways of Great Britain – II – Southern England* (London, 1961).

K. P. Witney, 'Kentish land measurements of the thirteenth century', *Archaeologia Cantiana*, cix (1992 for 1991), 29-39.

Index

www.ingramcontent.com/pod-product-compliance
Lightning Source LLC
Chambersburg PA
CBHW051309270326
41929CB00029B/3472